Animation Production

DOCUMENTATION AND ORGANIZATION

Animation
Production

DOCUMENTATION AND ORGANIZATION

Robert B. Musburger

CRC Press
Taylor & Francis Group
Boca Raton London New York

CRC Press is an imprint of the
Taylor & Francis Group, an **informa** business
A FOCAL PRESS BOOK

CRC Press
Taylor & Francis Group
6000 Broken Sound Parkway NW, Suite 300
Boca Raton, FL 33487-2742

International Standard Book Number-13: 978-1-138-03264-4 (Paperback)
978-1-138-08084-3 (Hardback)

Visit the Taylor & Francis Web site at
http://www.taylorandfrancis.com

and the CRC Press Web site at
http://www.crcpress.com

Printed and bound in the United States of America by Sheridan

To Pat—friend, companion, lover, wife, and the best possible in-house editor—for so many years of happiness in work, play, traveling, and living to the fullest.

Contents

Preface

This book has been prepared to fill a gap in the understanding of an often ignored or hidden aspect of animation production. Despite the appeal of sitting at a computer or drawing board and creating an award-winning animation without further thought, in reality, there are a variety of processes that should be considered and then accomplished during that process.

Part of the process of describing accurately this process, which I have labeled "Documentation," comes from the somewhat happenchance development of the art and skills of animation. The titles and uses of some of the documents described in this book vary among the many different styles and methods of producing animation. Kindly excuse the redundancy and contradiction in some of the details of this book.

An effort was made to indicate a reasonable, systematic approach for the use of various documents and forms described in this book. It starts with the basics of the original idea, continues with methods of developing that idea to the specifics of preparing and writing scripts, and completes the path with charts to assist in a logical path to actually start to create your animation. Handling sound and the final postproduction forms completes the listing of documentation and forms.

An extensive bibliography and listing of Internet sources to help you research your work, along with a glossary to define unfamiliar terms, complete this book.

Animation is a combination of art, technology, insightful creative thinking, and critical choices. Don't ignore any of those factors.

Good luck. I will watch for your acceptance of an Annie or an Oscar, as some of my other students did in the past.

Robert B. Musburger
Seattle, Washington

Acknowledgments

For 50 some years, I have been interested in, studied, and taught animation. I could not have accomplished what I have and been in the position to write this book if it were not for a lengthy list of people who in one way or another have supported me.

It would be impossible to recognize everyone, but those who come to mind include:

- *Former students*: Gregory Gutenko, Charley and Nancy Welborn, Karen Foss, Joe Tankersly, David Garfield, Dominic Sachse, Michael Carr, Roger Hull, George Greb, Gary Carder, Bill Vanatta, Liz Craig, Bob Basile, Susan Carter, and Clare Roberts.
- *Professionals*: Bob and Bill Wormington, and Murray Nolte from WDAF-TV days.
- *Faculty*: Sam Scott, Gaylord Marr, Elizabeth Czech-Beckerman, Tom Hoffer, Norm Medoff, Jennings Bryant, Ray Fielding, Ted Stanton, Mary Loy and Dick Brown, Jim Bray, and Beth Olson.

My relationship with Focal Press, in all of its iterations and owners, has stretched over 20 years with 4 books, 10 editions, and translations in Russian, Chinese, Spanish, and Portuguese. The books covered the topics of media writing, studio TV production, field video production, video news gathering, and animation production documentation. During that time, I have had the good fortune of working with at least 20 excellent editors, and for this book, Sean Connelly, Jessica Vega, Robert Sims, especially Viswanath Prasanna.

Author

Robert B. Musburger, PhD, was born and raised in Montana, grew up in Missouri and Kansas, and educated in Missouri, Kansas, Florida, Texas. He did his AS in Electronic Technology (1955–1956) in Central Technical Institute. He completed his BA in Speech-Theatre (1957–1961) in University of Missouri-Kansas City. He received his MA in Film History and Production (1974–1976) from University of Kansas and PhD in Telecommunication (1980–1983) from Florida State University. He has worked in publishing, aviation, legal, education, and media industries. He is working as a media consultant from July 2001. He has 40 years of experience in teaching radio–TV–film and animation at Avila College, University of Missouri—Kansas City, University of Kansas, Florida State University, University of Houston, and Washington Central University. He worked as a producer/director and production manager at WDAF-TV for 20 years. He is the writer/producer/director of more than 100 films, videos, animation, and multimedia productions. He worked as the host of interview programs on a commercial radio station in Houston, Texas, for 18 years. He is the founding member of KCUR-FM. As the owner and designer of Stained Pane Studios, he has 15 years of experience in windows, sculpture, lamps, and experimental graphic designs. He managed a country-rock band Carol Cruise and the Cruisers. He has authored five textbooks of 14 editions and translations in Chinese, Portuguese, Spanish, and Russian. He and his wife Pat have been together for 44 years. He fell in love and has planned on marking his final fini in the Pacific Northwest: Seattle, Washington.

Introduction to Animation Production Preparation

Kinetic Art is the first new category of art since prehistory. It took until this century to discover the art that moves. Had we taken the aesthetic qualities of sound as much for granted as we have taken those of motion, we would not now have music. But now in kinetic art and animation, we have begun to compose motion.

Len Lye (1964: 82)

Why is this Book Needed, and Why Should You Use It?

After years of teaching animation, working with animators, studying animation as an art form as a means of expression, and watching animation become a driving force in virtually all media forms, I felt I needed to add my thoughts. I decided to write to assist all of you interested in the field. Whether you want to create an animation production, study the animation as an art form, or simply love animation, my hope is that this book will give you an opening to fulfill those interests. At the same time, I have gathered the information in this book as a means to assist you, whether you are a student or a newcomer to the field. My goal is to unravel some of the mysteries of the many different documents used in planning and completing an animation project.

This book is written to give you a method of completing your goal of understanding the animation process in as professional a manner as possible within your capabilities. This book covers only a portion of the topics needed to completely understand all there is to learn about animation. My purpose is to tell you about a wide ranging and important aspect of the paper work, known as *documentation*. You need to learn to create and use documentation in order to move forward efficiently in the animation process.

This book *will not* cover the following animation topics: details of camera operation, lighting philosophy, editing, and the fine details of every computer application and program used in animation production and distribution. There are two reasons for ignoring these topics: First, an amazing number of books specializing in each of these areas individually and in great detail are available to you. Second, and most importantly, the rapid change in digital technology makes it almost impossible to accomplish my goal and report absolutely accurately on each aspect of animation and write a book like this one in the time book publishing requires.

Animation: A Definition

The definition of animation, for your understating of this book, includes such techniques as puppets, collages, sand and clay figures, found objects, painting and scratching on film stock, pin boards, time lapse, rotoscoping, silhouettes, and, of course, cel and computer animation. This broad definition is both a blessing and a detriment when you try to understand the creative process of animation. Traditionally, you could shoot a group of objects on video or film, or still shots, at the rate of one or two frames at a time to create animation. But today, with computer applications and digital equipment, no clear difference exists between a physical creation and a digital creation as a work of a creative animation project.

An early and specific definition of animation is that animation is utilizing the capability of the human brain to combine separate images into a continuous moving image by creating a series of drawings that relate into continuous flow of visual information.

Humankind has been interested in movement since the earliest artists painted on cave walls, on pottery, and on tombs of the dead. The key to movement in all media depends on the physical and psychological effects of the mental phenomenon of persistence of vision. Greek astronomers, Roman poets, and British, German, and Swiss scientists all were concerned with this mystery until the early 19th century. By the early 1800s, the fundamental principles of the mind and the eye's ability to connect more than one image after another into a continuous stream of visual material became better understood. For that mental leap, we now have motion pictures, video, and digital images.

One of the most quoted and accepted definitions of animation was stated by Norman McLaren of the National Film Board of Canada:

> Animation is not the art of drawings that move but the art of movements that are drawn; What happens between each frame is much more important than what exists on each frame; Animation is therefore the art of manipulating the invisible interstices that lie between the frames.
>
> **Furniss (1989: 3)**

Regardless of the animation definition that is published or accepted, animation will continue to be defined by technology, techniques, society, economics, politics, and the industry of show business. For you, it just means there are no limits to your creativity, but you must understand that the choices you make in your production, whichever technology you work within, must be comfortable to you.

History of Animation Production Processes

I will not bore you with a litany of dates, names, and inventions about the development of animation production. I would prefer to introduce you to and increase your curiosity about animation production processes, how it came to be, and how it exists now. In addition, I want you to understand you have a choice of spending all of your time experimenting with every production technique you can think of, or you may better spend your time studying what has happened before in the field of animation production. Use the skills and efforts made by your predecessors in developing, creating, and laying the groundwork of animation production; it has worked for 200 years, it can't all be outdated and useless.

Using strings of single images on a film strip base to animate objects preceded the development of the film itself. Many of the earliest films were produced to exhibit the so-called mysteries and special effects. In reality, they were "animated" before they were "filmed." To do so, early animators/filmmakers used single-frame exposure of action and artwork, and double exposures to create those effects. The fundamentals of animation and motion pictures developed from these same experimental techniques. Today, you may use the same basic techniques whether your production is created on film, video, or within a computer.

You will face the prospect of turning your ideas into a viable production acceptable to you and, just as important, acceptable and understood by your audience. You should start with a study of what has occurred before you in the field of animation. There is no point in your spending time and energy solving creative problems solved by others. Better you study the works of others to respect and understand how animators have created their works. The techniques they developed are still used in either analog or digital animation productions. You should watch examples of as many animators as you can, including all genres, styles, and formats. Especially watching animators who produced throughout the entire history of animation will give you a basis for building a solid foundation for your animation.

Reading about animators, their works, their lives, and the cultures within which they worked will provide you an understanding on how your life and your culture within which you live and work may affect your creative response. You must continue to read, study, and watch others to lay the groundwork to develop the production you want to do, and when completed, you will be proud to claim that as your creation.

Many fine books have been written covering the development of animation and how the animators solved their creative and technical concepts (see the Bibliography at the end of this book). Research other sources because the rapid technical changes in the field have never allowed the industry to stay in one spot and will continue to expand on a weekly, daily, and even hourly basis.

Introduction to Story Construction

In preparing to produce your animated production, you will be faced with organizing the planning of each step of the process. To assist in what could appear to be a complicated process, the focus of this chapter will lead you through a two-step analysis of describing each of the pieces of paperwork you may need to help you create your work. This chapter divides the needed documentation into two categories: descriptive documentation and form documentation. The differences sometimes may overlap, and depending on the individual processes used at each studio, the descriptive documentation and form documentation will vary in style, form, and use. The remainder of this chapter introduces the first step you need to consider mentally to start your production. You should start with your idea, then develop the concept, and, finally, move on to the rest of the story construction.

Chapter 2 covers the preliminary descriptive documentation you will need to understand and use to start organizing your production in order to develop your idea and concept as you concentrate on considering how you will move toward writing the script.

Chapter 3 includes the descriptive documentation for those stages needed to actually prepare your script. Chapter 4 deals with the method of script preparation.

Chapter 5 analyzes each specific form you may need or should use to better move your production forward efficiently and gives you full creative license to create your own concept. Chapter 6 concentrates on audio production and production forms you may use to lead to the final stages of the production process.

This chapter has been written to help you better understand the differences between the many types of documentation: descriptive and form documentations used in animation and in reality. This includes all methods of media production, audio, radio, television, cables, motion pictures, and satellite (Figure 1.1).

This chapter will include the exact process used in documenting an animated production. This chapter will also describe the documentation and forms you will need to use depending partially on the size of your production, the budget, the crew, and your client's desires. The following step-by-step process covers the critical areas, regardless of the complexity of your product. Several of the steps may be combined with other steps, again depending on the type of production you wish to create.

The documents you need to become familiar with and understand how to use during your production may include handwritten notes, outlines, storyboards, drawings, sketches, diagrams, or even conversations and notes from meetings among the crew or thoughts within your mind as the auteur.

Story Construction

The first step in creating a story that will become your animation production is constructing the story. In the past, the animator was the director, producer, and often even the actor and the writer because at first there were few scripts actually in place on paper during the animation production process. Animation was, and for you today might be, an auteur medium if you chose to write, direct, draw, render, and produce your animation concept.

Although during the earliest days of animation all of the writing aspects of the production process were completed by one or two people for any single production, the process of assembling the information needed for you to reach a complete production remains the same today, regardless of whether you or someone else actually writes the script or what form the written documentation becomes.

At the same time, a group of your crew may begin writing as a committee in a "gag" meeting. A "gag" meeting consists of three to a dozen writers, led by a producer. Their function is to work out a storyline, character development, and the scenes (gags) that build the action and the progress of the plot. With increased use of computers to create animation, the separation of writing and drawing became even more clearly defined. The value of quality writing in developing

```
┌─────────────────────────────────────────────────────────────┐
│                      DOCUMENT CHART                           │
├─────────────────────────────────────────────────────────────┤
│                                                               │
│                       DESCRIPTIONS                            │
│                                                               │
│                IDEA   PREMISE   CONCEPT   PLOT                 │
│                                                               │
│             OUTLINE   BIBLE LOGLINE/PROPOSAL                   │
│                                                               │
│                TREATMENT   DRAFT   SCRIPT                      │
│                                                               │
│                    CHARACTER STUDIES                          │
│                                                               │
├─────────────────────────────────────────────────────────────┤
│                                                               │
│                          FORMS                                │
│                                                               │
│       FIELD GUIDE   TIMING CHART   MOVEMENT CHART              │
│                                                               │
│          STORYBOARD   SCRIPT FORMATS   BUDGET                 │
│                                                               │
│          DOPE SHEET   CELL LIST   PLOT GRAPH                   │
│                                                               │
│      MODEL SHEET   ROUTE SHEET   EXPOSURE SHEET                │
│                                                               │
│   SHOOTING SHEET PROGRAM CHART   PRODUCTION BOOK               │
│                                                               │
│   STORYOUTLINE/PLOT GRAPH   GRATICULE/FIELD GUIDE             │
│                                                               │
│      COLOR ASSIGNMENTS   KEY FRAMES BACKGROUNDS                │
│                                                               │
├─────────────────────────────────────────────────────────────┤
│                                                               │
│                       AUDIO FORMS                             │
│                                                               │
│      BAR CHART LIP SYNC CHART   MOUTH SHAPES                   │
│                                                               │
│            SOUND TRACK   AUDIO ANALYSIS                       │
│                                                               │
│   PRODUCTION SCHEDULE   PRODUCTION FILES–FOLDERS              │
│                                                               │
└─────────────────────────────────────────────────────────────┘
```

Figure 1.1 Chart of Documents

The three types of documents described and explained in this chapter include descriptive documents, document forms, and audio document forms.

strong characters and stories to capture and hold the audience separates good writers from poor ones. All stories should be based on some kind of a conflict, but violence is not as important as the use of action that propels the audience into the story. Humor is crucial in most animation, even if a scene or two become serious with dramatic action. The success of the Pixar's animated films and Disney's features and shorts illustrates the value of well-constructed stories populated by believable characters, as opposed to the weak stories of some direct-to-video and television animation of today.

Summary

This chapter introduces you to the basic history and concepts of how animation has developed and how you may accept and use the definitive work of past animators. The first step in the process is to understand the many different documents and forms you need to learn to use to successfully complete your animation. A basic knowledge of story construction completes this chapter.

2

The Preliminary Descriptive Documentation of Animation

An Idea
A Concept
Story Considerations
Pace–Tempo–Rate–Rhythm
Stereotyping
Obscenity

Humor versus Drama
Action versus Violence
Settings
Genre
Summary

> Animation is not a genre! Animation is an art form and it can do any genre. It can do a detective story, a horror story, an R-rated story, or a kid's fairy tale. It doesn't do *one* thing it can do *anything*.
>
> **Bird (2004)**

Preparing for the production of animation starts with what seems to be a complex system of documentation. For ease in learning and using, the documentation may be separated into two categories: descriptive paperwork and production forms. This chapter deals with descriptive documentation that you should consider first.

Animation has no limits as to what the process may accomplish; therefore, your animation may use nonobjective and nonlinear plots and action sequences that live action finds difficult or impossible to complete without resorting to computer graphics imagery, which is also animation. Even though your animation should have a recognizable form, the beginning, middle, and ending patterns of a normal dramatic structure are not necessary in all cases. Audiences readily accept a more abstract pattern in animation storytelling than they do of live action.

In any story, there has to be a beginning, a middle, and an end. In animation, the beginning starts with an *idea*.

An Idea

A basic concept of what your production will do or say has to start with a simple idea. It could come from one of your personal experiences, from your observation of the world about you, or from brainstorming with others. Other possibilities

IDEA

Create a series of animated shorts to test how children react to different animation dramatic tools by showing two small space travelers enjoying a picnic on a new planet.

Figure 2.1 An Idea

An idea needs to be a short, concise description of the basic thought behind the project. Direct but precisely described to attract interest in the project.

may come from modifying an existing story by reversing images or characters, or by modernizing a myth, a fairy tale, or a traditional story. An excellent source for an idea may come from an event that happened to you, your family, friends, or crewmembers. And, there is always the possibility of you adapting a published work once you gain permission from the copyright holder (Figure 2.1).

A Concept

The philosophy behind a *concept* depends on ideas changed into action or incidents. A concept may start either as a function (a cat chases a mouse and captures it by grabbing it) or as a design where similar items are used differently (as capturing the mouse with a fish net). The two may be used together or as a contrast in a sequence of scenes. You may develop your concept around a central issue: political, cultural, national, or ethical, but it must involve action and characters with identifiable characteristics. Most importantly, develop a concept that is unique, you're telling a story that is told differently than you've seen elsewhere. Concept may be large and complicated or small and detailed to make a specific point. Concepts may also depend on associations: flowers may indicate the country, or love, or hay fever, depending on the plot (Figure 2.2).

Story Considerations

While converting your idea into a workable script, you might consider some of the following approaches to produce your best professional production. Think about what makes a better script: movement, humor, drama, action, violence, and stereotyping. Also keep in mind you must decide on settings, genre, and how you will develop your characters.

CONCEPT

The broadcast industry wants to learn what most attracts young viewers, violence, action, or humor. This concern came from heightened criticism of animation program produced specifically for children relying on violence rather than on any other dramatic form. A series of short animated sequences were produced using the same plot line but each of the four shorts used one of the three dramatic forms: violence, action, humor, and a third short is produced without any of the three dramatic forms as a control. Showing these shorts to a group of children while being observed by psychologists and communication specialists to record their reactions might help answer the question.

Figure 2.2 A Concept

Your concept should expand slightly from your description of your idea. It should include key action, major characters, locations, and if important time references.

Pace-Tempo-Rate-Rhythm

The perceived feeling of the passage of time in your animation depends on a sense of rapid motion. Animated productions control time better than live-action production because you control time with each individual frame. Therefore, in animation, time and the sense of passage of time become critical. Time is subjective, but the perception of time is controllable. For one audience member, a scene may appear to be moving rapidly, but for another, time passes at a much slower rate. The method of measuring time factors considers pace, tempo, rate, and rhythm.

Pace is the measurement of the perceived movement of the entire production during a specific period of time. *Tempo* is the specific rate of movement of an individual sequence or scene as expressed in music: largo, presto, and allegro. *Rate* is the perceived movement of time of individual performances, from short to long and anything in between. The perception of rate may be affected by the relationship between adjacent shots. *Rhythm* develops with variations in pace, tempo, and rate or any combination of such factors. Rhythm may be felt in the "beats" of a production (Figure 2.3).

Stereotyping

One danger in developing strong characters is that they may tempt you to rely on stereotyping. Stereotyping uses the technique of counting on the audience's preconceived notion of what a person or location will do because of the appearance of gender, ethnicity, religion, and economic or social status. Especially in animated shorts with limited time to develop three-dimensional (3-D) characters, you could use stereotyping to quickly establish a portion of a character's personality. The danger comes from using stereotypes in a negative manner, creating a character based on the worst negative characteristics of a group. Negative stereotypes must be avoided without harming your sequence. Instead, use stereotyping to quickly establish a location or some aspect of a character but remain with the positive characteristics not the negative ones. Avoid depicting any member of a group as having the same actions or personality characteristics attached to a group by extremists.

A writer must deal with the "isms"—racism, sexism, ageism, and, if you will, disabilityism. A difference exists between political correctness and depictions based on fairness and accuracy. Political correctness follows the law and the fashion of the moment, but you need to treat all individuals and groups of people with the same care and consideration you would expect to receive. We all are individuals, so we all must be respected for our individual characteristics.

Using stereotypes in a positive manner is often a necessity in media writing. In short timeframe productions, especially commercials and animation, you may use stereotypes to quickly establish mood, location, and descriptions of specific characters.

A police officer may be depicted as a short, stocky, red-haired Caucasian male in a blue uniform. That quickly tells the audience that he is an officer of the law without narration, labels, or other indication of the character because this has been the stereotype of a New York Irish policeman. It is not accurate, but virtually all audiences will accept and recognize the depiction without further explanation, which saves time. If the depiction is not negative, it is only sexist and can be avoided with creative planning on the rest of the scene.

MEDIA TIME MEASURES

PACE

THE PERCEIVED SPEED OF AN OVERALL PRODUCTION;

FAST–MEDIUM–SLOW

TEMPO

THE PERCEIVED SPEED OF INDIVIDUAL;

SEQUENCES OR SCENES

RATE

THE PERCEIVED SPEED OF INDIVIDUAL PERFORMANCE

SHOT LENGTH AND COMPARISON OF ADJACENT SHOT LENGTHS;

DEPENDING ON RELATIONSHIP TO ADJACENT SHOTS

RHYTHM

DEVELOPMENT OF VARIATIONS;

PACE, TEMPO, RATE, OR COMBINATION OF ALL THREE

AUDIENCE SENSES FLOW OF ACTION WITHIN:

SCENES, SEQUENCES, ENTIRE PRODUCTION

MAY BE CALCULATED IN "BEATS"—A MEASUREMENT OF LENGTHS OF

INDIVIDUAL SEGMENTS AND THE NUMBER OF SEGMENTS

IN A SEQUENCE

Figure 2.3 Chart of Time Factors

All aspects of media, in writing, shooting, and editing, may be analyzed using the four perceived measurements: pace, tempo, rate, and rhythm.

The danger of using stereotypes may lead you to choose negative characteristics or consistently create a character in a negative role specifically because of gender, sexual orientation, ethnicity, religion, or national origin. The tragedy of September 11, 2001, and the following unrest in much of the rest of the world should teach us all to carefully consider how we depict and think of people of other beliefs and backgrounds.

You must be even more careful in considering the depictions and treatment of people with individual differences. This extends to remembering women are not included in the term mankind rather than humankind and a fireman actually is a firefighter. If you use a person's physical condition, religious beliefs, age, or sexual persuasion in a story, it must be critical to the story, not used to categorize the subject of the story. Obviously, the use of slang expressions to describe groups of people is not acceptable except as a part of dialog to establish the personality of a character using the slang.

The tremendous power of the electronic media must never be forgotten as you place descriptions and develop characters in your stories and reporting. That power can cause far more harm than that can be imagined until an incident reveals that power in a negative manner.

Obscenity

Copywriters must take care that the shows they create do not offend the smallest portion of the audience possible. A critical measurement of offence is a material that might appear to be pornographic to any segment of the audience. Good taste and thoughtful consideration should guide you to avoid problems in this realm, but, inadvertently, and possibly from an effort to appeal to a specific segment of the audience, materials may fall within the categories of pornography.

The term "pornography" refers to any material that is sexually explicit and is intended to arouse the audience sexually. That is a very broad category, but the two specific areas of pornography of concern to you are sequences containing a material that is declared indecent or obscene. Any material is obscene if it is sexually explicit and offensive. Such a material is not protected by the First Amendment and may be prosecuted and punished for distribution in any manner.

The material declared indecent is not necessarily obscene and may be distributed on some media, but not broadcasting. Broadcasters are regulated by the Federal Communication Commission (FCC), which sets a continuously changing standard for what is indecent and cannot be broadcast without fines or threat of loss of the broadcaster's license. The same material may be distributed by cable, the Internet, or satellites without fear of retribution from the FCC at the present time.

Eighty percent of US households receive their broadcast signals over either cable or satellites, and an increasing number now receive programming from their computers and cell phones. However, few viewers know how to make the distinction between locally originated and broadcast network programming, broadcasting from cable, satellite programming, or the Internet. Also, you must be aware that obscenity and the definition of indecent varies between states and even individual cities and counties. Even more confusing is the definition differences between countries and cultures.

In the United States, the difference between indecent and obscene was set down by the Supreme Court in a 1973 case, *Miller v. California*, which defined obscene as any material fulfilling all three of the characteristics listed in Figure 2.4.

DEFINITION OF OBSCENE

According to 1973 US Supreme Court Case: *Miller v. California*

The decision was worded to define the difference between *"Indecent"* and *"Obscene"*

1. The average person, applying contemporary community standards, would find that the work, taken as a whole, appeals to the prurient interest.
2. The work depicts or describes in a patently offensive way sexual conduct specifically defined by the applicable state law.
3. The work, taken as a whole, lacks serious literary, artistic, political, or scientific value.

(State laws also apply to the second rule and may add more restrictions).

Since 1973 "contemporary community standards" have changed radically. Even more difficult for creators is the vast variation between "Applicable State Laws". What might be considered acceptable in California or Washington might be against state laws in Alabama, South Carolina, or Utah.

Figure 2.4 Definition of Obscene

To prevent unnecessary restrictions on the creative process, a producer, writer, or director of any media production must consider the laws defining obscenity, and more difficult, the state laws on obscenity.

Part of the problem for broadcasters is that their signal may cover a broad area of different cities, states, and even national regions that have varying community standards. Therefore, you must consider the lowest common denominator of standards when preparing copy for broadcast distribution. Your awareness of the distribution of whatever you create is critical. Edgier and more creative work may not be permissible on broadcast outlets, yet the same material could play to the same audience by cable, satellite, the web, or other Internet distribution systems with no fear of punishment or banning by the distributor.

Humor versus Drama

Humor, the basis of most but not all animation, is a subcategory of drama. All of the rules of dramatic structure hold true for humorous animation as well any other genre of drama. In many ways, you will find writing humor is much more difficult than writing straight drama.

In addition to all of the other requirements of a well-written drama, in a humorous production you must also appeal to the funny bones of the audience. The audience may be carried along with the strength of the animated characters, the believability of the plot, and the excitement of seeing a crisis develop and disappear, but most importantly, your audience must want to laugh, or at least be highly amused. The action and dialog need to either lead to or bring to an end a running joke or a comic situation.

Writing animation requires you to understand human and animal physiology and movement, as well as a strong sense of visual creativity. The visual may include not just the obvious actions of your characters, but their body movements, facial expressions, and physical relationships with your other characters.

Action versus Violence

Throughout the years of media distribution of entertainment programming, there has been the concern of the effects of violence on the audience. Of particular concern has been the effect on the younger audiences. The matter of violence on media has received special concern with the proliferation of computer games based on violent plots, characters, mistreatment of women, and action sequences. Unfortunately, with all of the concern and research, there is still no absolute conclusion connecting violent media with violent reactions or other harmful actions among young people.

While you consider the storyline of your project, you should consider the effects of unnecessary violence on your audience. You should also consider how any audience may value or criticize your work if it relies on gratuitous violence instead of quality plot, character, and action. Creating solid, meaningful concepts and carrying them without violence-filled action sequences is a lazy and useless method to cover poor creative thinking. You probably could replace the same violent scene with a carefully thought out and planned action scene.

Settings

Before you move too far into the process of your project, you need to consider where it is happening. Keep in mind, over 90% of what the audience sees at all times during a production is the background. The location, shape, and especially the color choices of the environment are critical to your production. Remember colors can set the mood and affect the emotions of the characters, and, as importantly, the emotional response of the audience.

Start simply, whether your story requires an internal location or an external location. If internal, you need to decide what kind of building are you thinking of (new or old), even a specific date, or time of day. Timing is also important. Not just the time of day, but the historical time of your production. If you set the scene outdoors in a forest, cityscape, or ocean, at a specific time period, make the scene consistent with the story you are telling. The costumes, makeup, and descriptions of your characters must match the choices you made in the settings.

The type of action your characters may be taking also needs to be considered when you choose your environment. Will they need large spaces, tight, confined spaces, or even undefined abstract space. When you produce a 3-D animation, the background becomes much more complex as you need to consider carefully the dimensionality of each setting and movement of the characters.

Your setting consists of the environment you want the action to take place in with all of the other elements, your characters, and in some cases changes in foreground elements such as clouds, fog, or smoke (Figure 2.5).

(a)

(b)

Figure 2.5

Pix of settings. (a) Exterior setting: An exterior setting could be simply clouds, sky, or some other abstract color, or a more detailed setting showing the type of environment you want your story be seen in. (b) Interior setting: Among other decisions you will make will be where physically you will place the action and characters of your story. It may be as simple as an abstract color or a detailed interior of a room or building.

Genre

As indicated in the quote from Brad Bird at the beginning of this chapter, the field of animation is not a genre, but animators may depict or use any genre format to tell their story. You should carefully choose what type of story you wish to tell. It may fall into any genre or even a combination of genre; as long as the combination makes sense to you, tells your story, and does not confuse the audience.

At the same time, do not place your characters in situations that don't make sense in relationship to your story and the goal you set in creating your animation. If you decide on a western genre, you can move beyond traditional western depictions, but don't suddenly create a sci-fi plot and story without making certain your writing and animation explain the jump in genre.

There is a nearly infinite list of literary and dramatic genre: drama, romance, mystery, horror, history, documentary, fantasy, as well as Western, Asian, satire, action, humor, action, or absurdist.

Summary

This chapter leads you through the primary documentation starting with your idea and how you will develop it with your concept. Some hints on developing your story with construction factors and timing are followed with controversies to carefully consider the topics "stereotyping" and "obscenity." This chapter wraps with hints on genre and uses a variety of dramatic tools to assist you in finalizing your project.

3

Documentation of Animation Preparation: Second Scene

A small child once said to me: "You don't draw Bugs Bunny, you draw pictures of Bugs Bunny." That's a very profound observation because it means that he thinks that the characters are alive, which, as far as I am concerned is true. And, I feel the same way about animation …. Animation isn't an illusion of life. It is life.

Chunk Jones (2002)

Now that the preliminary documentation in animation production has been covered, it is time to move on to the more identifiable documentation: The *Premise*, the *Plot*, the *Bible*, and the details of considering the story length, digital scripts, organizing your plans, and the character development for your story.

The Premise

The *Premise* must state in one sentence the entire concept, without dialog or narration. You reduce the idea to its simplest form. From this point, you develop and expand your idea without losing sight of the your original concept. If you can't summarize your idea in one concise statement, then you have not accurately thought about your concept. A premise is a description in one sentence listing the title, genre, characters, and the objective to be achieved. Plan your premise to attract the interest of others and influence others, especially supervisors and/or funders of the value of your concept and its value as a marketable creative production. The term *LogLine* is often used interchangeably with premise and follows the same definition.

Figure 3.1 A Premise

Similar to an idea, premise is a concise one-sentence description of your project, but with a little deeply approach than your idea description.

The premise should be written with the idea of expanding that document into a plan of detailed items: the plot and the bible, followed by consideration of story length and the development of the characters of the story. A carefully conceived *Premise* is necessary to present at any presentation to explore the possibility of funding that is expected or hoped for (Figure 3.1).

The Plot

Before your story may be told, you must take the idea, concept, and premise and develop a *Plot*. The plot and story develop around your key character as the center of the action. You should concentrate on a hero or a main character or an incident. The plot and characters must match or mesh, or they will distract the audience from following the plot. Write an outline or create a graph showing each key scene and how each sequence relates to other sequences. In moving your story forward, follow the golden rule of KISS "Keep It Simple and Succinct" and do not overwhelm the audience with words, but rather use the power of visuals to show the audience your story. Show the audience what is happening, with hints of coming actions before they occur so that the audience can be expecting something to happen and will be prepared to understand the gag.

Remember, in virtually all dramatic forms, including humor and action, a story may be broken down into three major parts: an exposition (describing characters and key action), a crisis stage, and then resolution and solving of the crisis. Once the concept is firmly in mind, then you must list the scenes addressing key plot points of the production. This acts as a guide to establish characters, locations, and basic actions. The outline may be expanded to provide a storyboard frame for each sequence of the outline.

Another approach you could use in your plot development would be a pattern of alternating dynamic and static sequences. As an example, a story starts with the characters in happy, satisfied relationships, with all going well (a static position); then, suddenly, something happens that destroys or threatens the relationship. It can be the intrusion of a new character or an old competitor, or even a physical change such as an earthquake. The plot now is in a dynamic position, and your protagonist (main character) must move the story to a new static position. Alternating between static and dynamic positions makes for an interesting manner of approaching and solving crises. A story may start in total dynamism, leaving you the challenge of creating stativity by the end of the production. Stativity does not necessarily mean a happy ending, but rather just an ending that satisfies the audience with the resolution of the primary crisis (Figure 3.2).

PLOT

Two young space travelers, Itsy and Bitsy, start off to explore a new planet. They fly successfully through space and land on the surface of the new planet. Using their space buggy, they explore the planet to find a lake where they plan to enjoy their lunch. They drive to their rocket in the space buggy and return home. This is the plot for the first "Control" short.

The next short will follow the same pattern except now Itsy and Bitsy will experience humorous events. Their space buggy is animated with a funny face, Itsy and Bitsy stumble around, cannot get nuts from a tree and are confronted by a weird fish while trying to find a spot for their lunch. They hurry back to the rocket and head home. This is the plot for the second "Humorous" short.

The third short follows the same pattern except everything Itsy and Bitsy do is full of action, moving rapidly, jumping around. They arrive at the lake, try to catch the fish, and fail while moving around a lot in the process. This the "Action" short.

The final short also follows exactly the same pattern as the first three shorts, but now every action is full of violence, including gratuitous and unnecessary violence. This short is the "Violence" short.

The four shorts will be shown to groups of small children with trained observers recording the children's reactions to each type of animation.

Figure 3.2 A Plot

A plot is a more detailed description of your project including descriptions of characters, actions, and more details on how you will explore your original idea and concept.

The Bible

The *Bible* should follow the description of your concept by being short, but with enough detailed information to clarify your plot outline. The stage that determines many aspects of an animated production is the bible. The bible is a listing of characters by name, complete description of their appearance, characteristics, personality, type of voice for casting, and most importantly, the relationship with other characters. You must also create a detailed list of locations, individual scene descriptions, all of the music you need, a complete list of each SFX (Special Effects), and a list of individual props. All of these detailed materials are required to provide the basis for planning backgrounds and other settings and the props you will need during the production (Figure 3.3).

The bible must include a summary of the concept and a summary of the critical plot points. Keep the descriptions brief but use this document to convince an audience, or possibly a funding source, that your idea has merits and you know what you are doing and how you will complete the project. You must also cover the format you plan to use, why that format is important, and how it adds to the quality of the production. Don't forget an educated calculation of the length of the finished production and an estimate of costs. Budgets are covered in the next chapter.

In this series of shorts, the characters are Itsy and Bitsy, non-gender specific young space explorers. Itsy is the pilot of the space rocket and space buggy, Bitsy is the navigator. Their voices are non human, but very understandable. They are very close buddies and co-explorers.

They start in space inside their rocket, land on the new planet, and emerge from the rocket in their space buggy. They travel to a lake where they plan on having a picnic for their lunch. On their way, they stop at a tree to gather nuts for part of their lunch. At the lake, a fish appears acting differently in each short depending on how Itsy and Bitsy try to catch it.

Each short will be approximately 3 minutes long. Each short will be shown to a different group of children to determine their reactions to the movement of Itsy and Bitsy. The research is designed to show if there is a difference in "attraction" and "likeabilty" between the dull control short, the humor short, the action short, and/or the violent short.

Figure 3.3 A Bible

The bible needs to fill in as many details as possible of what your story will look and sound like. It should include specifics about characters, actions, locations, and time relationships.

Story Length

The structure of an animated story will vary with the intended length. Animated shorts traditionally run 7, 11, or 22 minutes long. Three 7-minute, two 11-minute, or one 22-minute short makes up a half-an-hour of television programming. Animated features may run for 60–90 minutes long.

A 7-minute short consists of one act. You establish crisis and then resolve it, with a quick gag saving the main character. An 11-minute short moves with two acts. During the first act, you introduce a crisis or problem, with your character reacting setting up the first action. A short second act may contain a new crisis, but you resolve all of the story problems by the end of that segment.

A 22-minute short consists of three acts. The first is longest, to establish characters, location, and the basic storyline. Your conflict must be paramount in the first act. During the second act, your immediate crisis may be resolved, but unexpected changes in action introduce the major problem or a new crisis. The third act builds to a climax, followed by a resolution of all of the crises (Figure 3.4).

Features follow the same pattern as a 22-minute short, but each act lasts longer and becomes more complex as the story progresses, with increasingly more important or dangerous crises building to the final climax and resolution. You must increase the action rate as the plot progresses since animation is action and visually oriented media. The pace of action is critically important. A feature should include several subplots, some involving the main characters and some with secondary characters for added interest and comic relief. The action of features occurs in several different locations. You may change locations adding new interest and plot possibilities. A feature will also require you to develop many more characters than in a short, with different levels of importance to the plot and to the action. But each character must be defined and have a reason for existing in the production to help move the plot forward, directly or indirectly.

ANIMATION STORY LENGTH

Internet animation   As short as 5 seconds, as long as animator wants

Individual shorts   3:00–7:00–11:00 minutes

Story shorts   22:00–30:00–45:00 minutes

TV half-hour program   3–7:00, 2–11:00, or 1–22 minutes short

Features   Anywhere from 60–90 minutes

ACT PLANNING

7:00 or shorter One act: all story developments introduced and resolved

11:00 Two acts: 1st act crisis introduced, but end of 2nd act all resolved

22:00 or longer, Three acts, 1st act conflict introduced, characters, action explained, 2nd act crisis may be resolved but new problems are introduced, 3rd act builds to a climax and all matters are resolved.

Figure 3.4 Story Length Chart

The chief determinations of the length of your story depend on your concept, your budget, and your distribution plan. The genre of the story you want to tell and who your predicted audience may be also will control the length of your production.

Direct-to-video productions vary from features originally released for public theatres in that they are produced with smaller budgets, are often shorter in length, and have lower production values. As studio marketers become aware of the income value of direct-to-video, the production values and the care taken in producing these quick-to-market animation features and packages of shorts should improve.

Internet animation generally uses shorter formats and less complicated production techniques. Internet animation may be as short as 5–10 seconds, or as long as you want it to be (Figure 3.4).

Digital Script Writing

Digital technology has provided today's writer with unrestricted means of telling their story. Now, there is no limit to what either a digital or film production crew can produce using the latest and yet to be developed digital technology.

Scripts used by producers of the mini-dramas distributed via the Internet follow whichever medium the producers used to create the original before distribution. As the popularity of Internet distribution and distribution for mini-screens on cell phones, PDAs, and iPods increases earning a profit, unique methods of creating the dramas will develop. With that development will come changes in formats paralleling the changes that occurred as film, radio, and television which found their audience and market. Now, those who are preparing scripts for the new digital media will use the format they have used to create analog or digital productions or are familiar enough to use comfortably. The production unit or the funding source may determine the choice.

Multimedia, Internet, and Web page scripts have not been formalized in the same way as scripts for other electronic media. Digital scripts take a variety of forms, some borrowing from both motion pictures and video as well as from audio–video script formats. The problem of indicating branching, choices for interaction, and the variety of different media used in one digital production requires a specialized script tailored to the specific production. The script must contain enough information for the producer/director to understand what is required to assemble the segments. The editor must also be instructed on the specifics of chapter assignments, transitions, linking, and other specialized techniques in a digital interactive production.

Character Development

As the writer, you must concentrate on developing characters and action scenes. Even though action, movement, and the visuals provide the key to pleasing an audience in animation production, you must properly develop characters that the audience wants to believe in, or at least believe fit the plot. In every drama, including animation, whether the plot is serious or comic, a conflict must exist or be created. The conflict depends on the relationship between an antagonist and a protagonist. The antagonist may be a natural event, a human, or a machine, depending on your decisions and the direction of the plot. The antagonist will oppose the protagonist, the main character of the plot, providing the crisis or the conflict necessary for a drama.

If you animate humanized characters, animals, creatures from space, or mythological figures, they must communicate among themselves as if they were humans so that the human audience can relate to the characters and understand why the relationships exist and why the actions develop as they do. There must be recognizable, strong personalities that are good, bad, or in between, but they also must be characters who the audience can accept as existing within the storyline of the production. Some characters will dominate the plot, and others will be subservient or neutral, but all characterization must be clear enough for the audience to understand exactly what type of personality a given character exhibits.

All of your characters must be recognizable to the targeted audience. Whether the audience is children watching morning or afternoon television, primetime or late-night adult viewers, or casual viewers, the character must make sense to the audience. The direction the character moves in the story and the motivation for that movement let the audience feel part of the story through their understanding of what is happening and what might happen next. Anticipation keeps an audience interested and tuned to the program. Your characters must also grow to show a change in how they have felt, learned, or reacted to others in the cast and to the actions that occur to them as individuals.

Some of the basic recognizable traits of characters are age, physical size, strength, appearance, gender, and relationship to others as a leader, follower, or sidekick. Your animation production depends upon at least one character taking a leadership role. An animated series requires a leader plus a leader's sidekick or buddy. That side-kick may be a goof-off, a devoted friend, or an idiot, but the story's action needs to show a contrast between the lead character and the supporting character or characters.

When you develop a three-dimensional character, they will show intelligence, stupidity, like ability, loyalty, destructiveness, dejection, supportiveness, uncooperativeness, aloofness, friendliness, unpredictability, or predictability, or a combination of several of these traits. Without such recognizable traits, the characters become two-dimensional cardboard cut-outs (Figure 3.5).

Character development depends equally on both the physical and psychological actions of your characters: how they look, how they move, and also most importantly, what made them look as they do and why they moved the way they did. Motivation and explanations of actions tell the audience what you are trying to illustrate with the movements and relationships of the characters. Keep cast as simple as possible, but be consistent for the script. Do not describe your characters using formula, each should stand out as an individual but appear as an ensemble without creating stereotypical actions or dialog.

To create the best possible acting performance of your characters, you need to become that character to help you decide how to make the character appear to do what you want it to do. Try to feel what that character feels, how they respond to the actions you have designed for them, and how they react to other characters and situations you created in the story.

How characters speak, what lines you write for them, depends on who you have intended that character to be. That will partly be dependent on your objectives in telling your story and the objectives you are aiming for in the story (Figure 3.6).

Model Sheets

You will need to create model sheets for each of the characters. A model sheet consists of pencil drawings or a computer file of a character in different poses viewed from different angles, as well as close-ups (CU) of the head, hands, and other distinguishing body parts. Sheets need to be made of each costume and also of critical props. Each character may have a selection of mouth shapes, characteristic emotional facile and body shapes, and walk cycles.

The model sheet guides the many different artists involved in the production to maintain consistency in drawing each character. The collection of drawings of the model sheets may also be labeled "Character Pack" (Figure 3.6).

Production Chart/Book

By the time you have reached this point in working on your animation, you should organize all of the documents you have used in the process. This includes all written material, starting with your idea, concept, treatment copies of storyboards, notes, emails, and hard copies and digital files you have created or received. If you have created a multitude of documents on one subject, for instance, a dope sheet for each shot or sequence, they should be bound in groups and filed in order so you may quickly review your process at that point.

This record will be valuable to you for two reasons: One, it provides a detailed account of what you have accomplished, or tried to accomplish while working on your project. This record will allow you to go back and check each step you performed in case there is a problem and your work hasn't turned out the way you had hoped it would. This allows you to go back and correct the problem and continue to finish your project.

Figure 3.5 Model Sheet

A key factor in the success of your story will be the believability and accuracy of how you develop; who your characters are; and how they act, speak, and relate to the other characters and the environment you placed all of them in.

```
┌─────────────────────────────────────────────────────────────┐
│                    DEVELOPED CHARACTERS                       │
│                                                               │
│   DISNEY                                                      │
│          Mickey Mouse, Private Snafu, Buzz Lightyear          │
│                                                               │
│   WARNER BROS.  (Chuck Jones)                                 │
│          Bugs Bunny, Elmer Fudd, Daffy Duck                   │
│                                                               │
│   FLEISCHER                                                   │
│          Betty Boop, Superman, Popeye, Koko the Clown         │
│                                                               │
│   TERRY, LANTZ                                                │
│          Mighty Mouse, Woody Woodpecker                       │
│                                                               │
│   BUD FISHER                                                  │
│          Mutt and Jeff, Krazy Kat                             │
│                                                               │
│   COLUMBIA                                                    │
│          Gerald McBoing-Boing, Mr. Magoo                      │
│                                                               │
│   DREAMWORKS                                                  │
│          Shrek                                                │
│                                                               │
│   ANIME                                                       │
│          Godzilla, Princess Mononoke                          │
│                                                               │
│   AARDMAN                                                     │
│          Wallace and Gromit                                   │
│                                                               │
│   INDEPENDENT                                                 │
│          The Grinch, Rocky & Bullwinkle, Caroline, Prince Achmed │
└─────────────────────────────────────────────────────────────┘
```

Figure 3.6 Developed Characters

The second value to this book is the record you may use in the future as you work on other animation projects. You may review what you did on this project, maybe reveal some areas you will do differently and other areas where you were very successful and you would like to repeat. Remember that the best way to learn is by carefully considering your errors and mistakes and not repeating them.

The next step in the animation production process is to organize all of the information gathered so far and create a *Production Book*. The management of any animation project, regardless of the size, complexity, or scope, needs to be organized. Even if your crew is one-person (you), that person needs to have all of the known details of the production written out so that nothing will be forgotten or misplaced in the order of the production.

Your production book should include all of the documents as they are created along with changes and additions. An important item in the book is your production schedule. Once developed, your storyboards also need to be included. A production book is an obvious place to record notes, emails, texts, or any other written communication concerning your production. Essentially, a production book should become a detailed diary of the work you perform to create your animation. These notes may be helpful on this project as well as on your next project.

A well-designed and followed production book may be an important element in your ability to become an efficient production manager. Within

SCENE#	B/G	FRAMES	CONTENT	SET	COMPLETION DATES			
					Blocking	Animation	LipSync	Rend
			PRODUCTION TITLE					
CLIENT								
EPISODE								
1	Sky	120	Rocket enters FR-L					
1A	R-Int	30	Itsy & Bitsy in rocket cockpit					
2	Sky	50	Rocket approaches plant					
3	A	15	Rocket lands					
4	A	10	Space buggy appears					
5	A	10	Buggy moves to right, Itsy & Bitsy aboard					
6	B	5	CU-Itsy & Bitsy talking					
7	A	25	I & B in buggy move right					
8	C	25	I & B approach Tree					
9	C	50	I & B try to harvest nuts					
10	C	15	I & B move right in Buggy					
11	D	40	I & B approach lake					
12	D	50	I & B discuss picnic site					
13	D	25	I & B set up picnic					
14	E	30	Fish leaps from water					
15	F	50	I & B discuss catching the fish					
16	F	15	I & B try to catch fish and fail					
17	D	25	I & B pick up the picnic					
18	D	15	I & B get in buggy					
19	A	10	I & B in buggy move left					
20	A	15	Buggy pulls in the rocket					
21	A	20	Rocket takes off					
22	Sky	50	Rocket travels through space					
23	Sky	50	Rocket disappears into space					
24								
25			END SHORT # i					
26								

(a)

Figure 3.7

(a) Production Book

(Continued)

```
PRODUCTION BOOK CONTENTS


                    Copies of each of the following:

Your idea                           Exposure sheet

The concept                         Background list and examples

The premise and/or logline          Key frames

The plot                            Program chart

The bible                           Route sheet

Descriptions of all characters      Color chart, examples

Proposal                            Production book

Treatment  (each version)           Time frame chart

Each outline                        Dope sheet

Your budget                         Audio analysis chart

Production chart                    Bar sheet

Each storyboard                     Dubbing chart

Each script draft                   Lip Sync chart

Model sheet                         Production schedule

Each copy of each script draft      Production folder

Flow chart                          All memos, notes, emails, messages

Movement chart
```

(b)

Figure 3.7 (Cotinued)

(b) Production Chart

professional studios, a *Production Chart* is often tied to the production book. The chart will lay out for you step by step the order specific items need to be completed, even down to individual frames and sequences. Such a chart may not be necessary for your first short, but if you plan on working in a professional studio, don't be surprised if you are expected to create and follow such a chart (Figure 3.7).

Summary

This chapter details the first three critical stages of preparing your animation production after you decided what your idea is and how you will expand and develop that idea with your concept. Now you will write your Premise, expand it in your Plot, and then write your Bible. This chapter also discusses how to determine the timing of the production, digital timing differences, and suggestions on assembling the documentation needed to create a log of all of your work and a plan to keep the project moving in the direction you want it to move, and how to develop the very characters who will inhabit your animation.

4

Narrative Documents for Animation Production

Manual construction of images in digital cinema represents a return to 19th century pre-cinematic practices, when images were hand-painted and hand-animated. At the turn of the 20th century, cinema was to delegate these manual techniques to animation and define itself as a recording medium. As cinema enters the digital age, these techniques are becoming commonplace in the film-making process. Consequently, cinema can no longer be clearly distinguished from animation, it is no longer an indexical media technology but, rather, a sub-genre of painting.

Lev Manovich (2016)

Once you develop beyond the concept stage and you write the *Premise,* the *Bible,* work on developing the story length, then you organizing the development of the *Characters* you create the next series of documents. You will start with the *Log Line, Proposal, Treatment,* followed by the *Story Outline.* Remember Log Line and Premise are often used interchangeably. Finally, work on the *Drafts* which you work on to clarify your original thoughts.

The Proposal and the Log Line

Log Line

A log line is a tool used by animators to "sell" their idea or concept. The log line may sound like it is a TV commercial, but it is sales pitch, just like a TV commercial. The log line should be limited to no more than three sentences. It needs to be very brief but written with precise and colorful language that will hold the

Figure 4.1 Log Line

Similar to a concept, a log line is intended as sales point included in a pitch session to convince fund raisers or sponsors of the validity of your concept and ability to produce the animation you want to complete.

attention of the listener. The ability to receive funding or distribution may rest on the proper and well thought out log line (Figure 4.1).

Proposal

Your proposal is a sales tool to provide the potential fund source, a rational for loaning the funds for the production. At some point, you must decide who will pay for the production. Even if you plan on self-producing, you must work out a budget, at least tentatively. If it is not self-produced, then you will need to convince someone or some organization to provide the funding.

Your proposal should be no longer than two pages. You need to describe what the production will look like, without dialog or narration, and you *should* provide the briefest of scene descriptions. The descriptions should reflect your concept, accurately, but without final detail. Your approximate budget should include a timeline, outlining the progression of the production day by day, from scripting through to the completed film or computer file. You should prepare both a proposal and budget and present both together at the same time (Figure 4.2).

PROPOSAL

Two gender neutral space creatures Itsy and Bitsy take off in their space ship to explore a new planet. They manage to crash-land their rocket without harming themselves. They unload their space rover to explore the new planet. They must find a way through a big mountain to find a suitable location for a picnic lunch. On the way, they meet and try to capture a large butterfly, but failed. The search for a picnic site leads them to a lake full of fish, which they try and fail to catch. Fortunately, they brought their lunch and managed to consume it before it is time to return to their space rocket and find their way back to their home planet. Each of the four 3-minute episodes will be filled with different levels of humor, violence, or action as the basis for a study of the reaction of young children to the three stimuli.

A budget of approximately $4,000 will cover the cost of materials to create cel-animated episodes. Labor costs will require $10,000 and finishing another $2,000. The project will be completed within nine months of final acceptance of scripts and approval of financing. Writing scripts will require approximately 6 months from approval of the treatment. The episodes will be shot on film or will be distributed via either film or a digital medium.

Figure 4.2 Proposal Sample

A full description of your animation, but limit it to two pages, if possible. It should completely describe your project, but avoid narration or dialog. This document is also used to convince fund sources of the value of your concept.

Treatment

Your treatment is a narrative description of the project, brief but comprehensive. Though not a script, it should follow the order of the script. Once you have decided on all of the characters and details of the production, then you write a complete description of the production as your treatment, with no dialog, and avoid technical media or animation terminology. Your treatment must include brief descriptions of key characters; brief descriptions of each sequence or scenes, depending on the length of your production; and a brief description of the action you plan each of your characters to perform without detailed dialog. You only mention special effects if it is essential to understand your concept. Your treatment should adopt a short-story format adopting a lively prose style that dramatizes the basic premise and yet effectively communicates the tone and flavor of the story. If your production is to be a game or a portion of a game, the treatment needs to describe the game's segment, each stage, action, and variations in flowcharts.

The treatment must fully describe the action, movement, visuals, graphics, and type of dialog without specific shots, or transitions. The idea behind your treatment is to create a document that may be read and comprehended by a nonmedia person who, once finished reading the treatment, should be able to visualize and understand what your production will look and sound like. This document must also be approved and signed by all who may have any authority over financing and the finished work before proceeding to the first script drafts.

Your treatment is an important step in the development of a script. You should write it in the third person, present tense. You visualize the story as it will unfold on the screen and give a play-by-play of all major actions and scenes in reduced form. You compose the treatment with the hope you may receive an approval or commission to write the script. A poorly written treatment may very well sink the concept before it moves any closer to completion. A treatment is not a legal document fashioned with dry regularity and precision. It must excite and interest a producer or funding source and serve as a thorough and helpful guide for the writing of your script or screenplay. Your treatment provides some protection against future writing problems by forcing you to resolve many story and character difficulties prior to actual scriptwriting. If you plan for external funding, the treatment accompanies the proposal to the pitch (Figure 4.3).

The Pitch

A pitch is a meeting with the potential funding source. To gain funding, you may be required to perform a "pitch" session. At that time, you will stand in front of the developer or producer and describe to the point of acting out the entire animation. Depending on your enthusiasm and ability to describe your concept, you may or may not win the pitch session and walk away with or without the assignment and funds you need to move onward. Your pitch session starts with researching your client and your potential audience. Learn what their operation (company, network, distributor) uses now and is looking for now. Remember, these people live very busy lives with very little time to waste. Prepare to make your presentation on time, orderly, and to the point. You should be able to describe your animation in 5 minutes, 10 at most. Cover the critical points: plot, key characters, genre, your intended audience, and the reason your production ought to be financed or distributed.

TREATMENT

In order to better test the relative response of children to various elements in television cartoons, it is necessary to produce a specific controlled series of cartoons, rather than using animation presently being telecast. In order to produce such materials, it is important to make them as close as possible in appearance and quality as those presently telecast.

This project will produce four 3-minute cartoons using the same story line, but varying the activities of the characters to create one episode that has no action, violence, or humor. The second will use action without gratuitous violence or humor, the third will be based on children's humor without action or violence, and the fourth will feature gratuitous violence without any humor or action aside from the violence.

The treatment for the neutral episode follows:

A small planet appears and a space ship approaches from a distance. Itsy and Bitsy are sitting at the controls. They discuss the likelihood of landing on the planet and decide it looks safe. They remember to buckle their seat belts and the space ship lands on the planet. Once the spaceship comes to a stop, they drive out in the Space Rover, a two-seat vehicle designed for exploring planets.

They discuss which way to go and agree on a direction and away they go.

They are pleased with the beauty of the planet passing mountains, rivers, and a lake. They decide that the lake will be a good spot to have their lunch. They pull up to the lake, get out, and Itsy spreads a blanket for a place to eat. While they are eating, a large butterfly flutters right by them as they sit on the blanket. They admire the butterfly and then decide to find some desert. They discover a nut tree and decide if they shake it gently some nuts will fall out of the tree for their desert. They pick up some nuts and find them crunchy and delicious. Suddenly, they see a fish jumping in the lake. After watching the fish for awhile, they decide it is time to return home. They load up the Space Rover and head back to the space ship. Once the Space Rover is inside the rocket, they take off and fly into the sunset.

Figure 4.3 Treatment

The treatment describes the entire production in greater detail than the proposal, using a narrative format without technical jargon. The treatment should tell the story as if it were a short story without dialog.

You leave the proposal, budget, and treatment with the funding source as a reminder of how you propose to spend their money. The next meeting with your funding source will involve the writing and acceptance of a firm contract as written. The treatment provides the important second step in the sales presentation for funding and the first step in creating a draft script.

Make certain the audience received a copy of your treatment and bring extra copies with you. Wait for questions, answer them briefly and to the point. Learn to read your audience. Your pre-pitch research will give you much of the information you need to know who your audience is and what they may be looking for. Good luck.

Animation Plot Outline/Graph

An outline or plot graph includes a listing of key points of the story, indicating the start, middle, and the ending. You need to create sketches of key scenes, but details are added later in scripts or treatments. Key characters and scenes may be included if critical to the design of the story. Your story outline essentially provides a list of the key aspects of your production written in an outline form.

This project consists of four short, 3-minute animations: one boring, one humorous, one active, and one violent.

A small space rocket shoots across space toward a mystery planet.

Two space explorers, Itsy and Bitsy, fly the rocket.

The rocket approaches and lands on the mystery planet.

A two-person space buggy emerges down a ramp driven by Itsy and Bitsy.

The space buggy crosses the surface of the planet, stops at a tree.

Depending on which short, the space explorers harvest the nuts.

Either they find the nuts suitable, or not, or impossible to harvest.

From the tree, Itsy and Bitsy travel to a lake.

In some of the shorts, there is a fish they either catch it or not.

Giving up on the fish, Itsy and Bitsy head back to the rocket on the buggy.

The buggy goes up the ramp and the rocket takes off and flies off into space.

Figure 4.4 Outline

A list of critical scenes to be included in your animation to illustrate how you are going to tell your story.

This form allows a reader or potential producer to quickly scan your concept and make a quick decision. Writing your animation outline gives you the opportunity to think of your production in terms of "Beats." Decide how you plan on creating the flow and rhythm of your idea, introducing your characters, the conflict, and the resolution all are a matter of timing, or what is commonly called the "Story Arc." "Beats" refers to creating a production that has a sense of rhythm to it like a good jazz musical number. The beats may vary, but the beats help the audience feel the sense of what you are trying to show them.

The same material may be entered into a Plot Graph that summarizes the aspects of your animation for accurate and efficient consideration and decision from the viewer. Such a graph may be created on a computer application like XLR (Figure 4.4).

Budget

You are responsible for the treatment, but the budget more likely will be the responsibility of the producer. Keep in mind that whatever you as the writer put on paper will affect the cost of the production. You need to be aware of budgeting only as an overall variable of the production. Whatever you have in mind for your production may or may not affect the cost of the production. You constantly will need to make decisions between costs and creative requirements of your production. One of the worst animation nightmares is running out of funds before you complete your production.

Complex and expensive locations should be avoided unless there is a budget specifically set up for such locations. A fly-by of Mount Fuji in Japan may sound like a clever idea, but unless stock footage may be found, it is beyond most any corporate budget unless that company has an office sitting in front of the mountain.

Two methods for maintaining control over production costs may be used. In the first method, your production unit is a self-contained, individually budgeted unit within the company. The unit fulfills requests to complete productions on an as-available basis until the production unit's budget for the year has been expended. This places you in an awkward position of either accepting a simpler and cheaper production or accepting an expensive project. This method parallels the methods most students must use in their early animation projects. Generally, such production units are controlled by and the selection of projects come from a higher level of management who must make the decisions of setting priorities for project selection.

The second method, the charge-back system, is a method of "paying for" a media production unit within a production. Each item you need or want in your production requires you to submit a request for a proposal (RFP) stating what you want done. The production unit then studies the request, performs preliminary research, and issues a proposal, treatment, and budget. This RFP must include costs for equipment, labor, rentals, both hardware and software, studio time, travel, and special effects. This allows you to work only on productions that a department really wants or needs and can afford. It also equalizes the responsibility between you and the fund supplier.

Budgets may be written in several forms: a Preliminary Budget written to estimate the costs for your production, followed by an Adjusted Budget to accommodate changes. And the final Production Budget becomes the document both you and the funding source will follow carefully. You may write your budget as a one-page format, but a professional budget may run as long as 10 pages in great detail (Figure 4.5).

Story Boards

A *Storyboard* is a series of drawn frames or pictures. Each represents a single shot or sequence, panel by panel, of an animation giving the creator and the rest of the team a way to conceptualize what is intended in the production. Whether you create the storyboard before or after you write the script depends on the size of your production or the policy of the studio or school. As an individual producer, you should create the two simultaneously if possible, since your story development and storyboard affect each other.

Historically, Disney developed the "factory" system of producing animation beginning in the 1930s by creating individual departments including separate scriptwriting and storyboard departments. Other studios used storyboards in many different ways, but the basis for each use was to visually organize the production for all to view. For some writers, drawing storyboards was not a problem, since most early animators were artists, but with time, storyboard creation became an art in itself.

The first addition to your duties as a writer is to create storyboards, or at least sketches, of each scene before the cels are drawn or computer files created. In addition to the drawn frames, you will add indications of dialog, camera and character movement, sound, music, frame, and scene numbers.

As the storyboard artist, you must accept the responsibilities of the director, interpreting the script, drawing each scene, and even drawing key frames and individual cels. As the storyboard artist, you may also decide on the movement of both the characters and the camera. The ability to draw boards and to maintain the vision of your original concept is critical for quality animation productions.

The first stage is to sketch roughs of each frame called *Thumbnails*, small drawings designed to fit the entire sequence on one page. The next stage occurs after the director (or you) make changes and the storyboards are now called *Rough Pass*. This version shows each panel much larger and in greater detail. Next, the

CREW	# DAYS	COST	TOTAL COST	TOTALS
Terry	20		$1,000.00	
Louise	15		$500.00	
Jeffry	30		$750.00	
Susan	40		$900.00	
Mary	10		$400.00	
Sam	5			
		PRE-PROD. TOTAL		$3,550.00
Melissa	15		$450.00	
George	15		$450.00	
Alfredo	50		$500.00	
Lois	5		$100.00	
Fernando	5		$100.00	
		PROD. TOTAL		$1,600.00
Pat	10		$400.00	
Leo	5		$200.00	
Brent	5		$200.00	
Hernandez	35		$450.00	
Ali-Fez	35		$500.00	
Samuel	5		$400.00	
		POST PROD. TOTAL		$2,150.00
			$5,000.00	
			$1,000.00	
			$100.00	
			$200.00	
			$6,300.00	
		OVERHEADS TOTAL		$12,600.00
				$3,000.00
		COST TOTAL		$22,900.00
		TAXES		$500.00
15%		GRAND TOTAL		$26,400.00

(a)

Figure 4.5

(a) A Simple Budget Form. A budget for a small or simple production needs to list the key areas of expenditures and estimated costs. It may be designed to list costs by the day labor costs, equipment costs, and/or rental costs. But, it must be as accurate as possible to consider to show you what the costs may be as well as to explain to a sponsor how their money will be spent. *(Continued)*

PRODUCTION TITLE						
Account #	PERSONNEL	COST	RATE	TOTAL		PostProd+Sound
1000	Producer				5000	Post Super
1001	Director				5001	Editor
1002	Designer				5002	Asst Edit
1003	TD				5003	Composer
1004	Viz Direct				5004	Musicians
1005	Prod. Asst				5005	Voice Director
					5006	Mixer/Edit
	Animation Crew				5007	Studio Engineer
2000	Director					
2001	Layout					Equip Rental
2002	Character Design				6000	Camera
2003	Story Board				6001	Sound Equip
2004	Art Super				6002	Grip Rental
2005	Art Asst				6003	Sound Record
2006	Rotoscoper				6004	VTR/Digital
2007	Digital Art				6005	Animation Cam
2008	Background Art				6006	Pencil Test Cam
2009						
	Studio Crew					Digital Equip
3000	Direct Photography				7000	Paint Station
3001	Cam Operator				7001	Scan Work Station
3002	Asst Cam Oper				7002	Composite Station
3003	Set Designer				7003	Graphics
3004	Prop Builder				7004	File Storage
3005	Gaffer				7005	Motion Capture
3006	Grip				7006	Equip Storage
					7007	Performance Suite
	Talent					
4000	Writer					Art Supplies
4001	On-cam Principle				8000	Paper/Paint
4002	Voice				8001	Brushes
4003	Audition Costs				8002	Graphics
4004	Casting Director				8003	Type Setting
					8004	Cam Supplies
					8005	Ink & Paint Service
					8006	Storage

This is a small list of individual items that must be calculated and kept track of during any major production.

(b)

Figure 4.5 (Continued)

(b) A Page of a Complex Budget Form. A professional budget form may run from 5 to 10 pages. Each expenditure is coded with a number to help keep track or where money is spent and by whom it is spent. To be of any value, it must be accurate during planning and during production as an accurate record of all expenditures.

boards are cleaned up, corrected with everyone in the production, including lawyers accepting the work. Now, they are labeled as the *Final Pass* with dialog, sound, and other data added.

You may find it helpful to take your final pass boards, cut them out, and create a flipbook of your production. This creates a handy easy-to-view source for you and all of those involved in your project. It's a chance to see what and how the project appears in motion (Figure 4.6).

It will be changed and updated as the project moves forward. Its main responsibility is to keep everyone, from the director to the crew informed as to what is planned and how it will be accomplished.

Animatic/Leica Reel/Pre-Viz

Once you complete your storyboard, at least the first draft, you should consider creating an animatic. An animatic is a recording of your animation. An older term for the same operation was called a Leica Reel in honor of the German still 35 mm camera, originally used to photograph storyboards. The purpose of your animatic is to give you a realistic view of what your idea may look and sound like once it is completed. Carefully thinking about your concept by observing

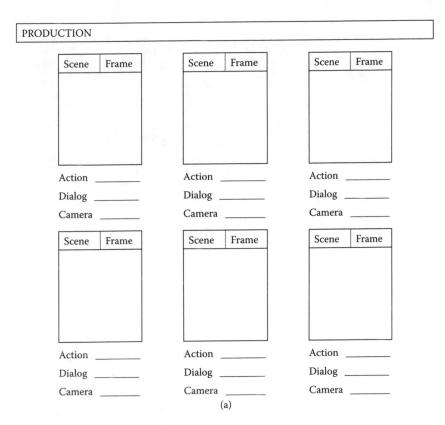

(a)

Figure 4.6 (a and b) Examples of Story Boards

Storyboards may take a wild range of forms. But, at its simplest it should be detailed enough to offer all involved the information needed.   *(Continued)*

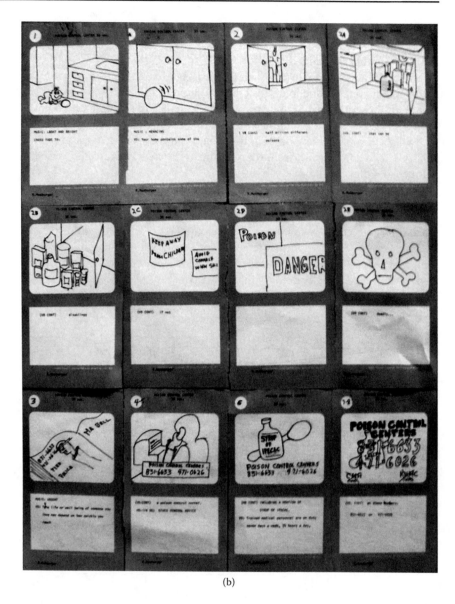

(b)

Figure 4.6 (Continued) (a and b) Examples of Story Boards

Storyboards may take a wild range of forms. But, at its simplest it should be detailed enough to offer all involved the information needed.

the single frames of your storyboard is important, but that does not give you the same sense of timing and the flow of your production that your animatic will give you. One method of producing your animatic is to record your sound track using a computer application such as Premier. Then, add single shots of your storyboard frames to match the sound track. Don't forget to allow for music and effects, if those factors are important to your story. Another method is to record all of the frames of your storyboard using a computer application. Then, you need to time how long each frame should last by reading your script, also allowing for music and effects and adjusting the length of each frame accordingly.

In the production of live-action media, a process labeled *Pre-Viz* basically uses the same process as an animatic for an animated production. Each section of live action is created on a computer, shot with a still camera, or captured from test footage. Once assembled, the Pre-Viz gives the director the same benefits an animation director receives from viewing an animatic.

Drafts

The First Draft

You begin your script writing with a *First Draft* to organize your idea, concept, and thoughts. You write the first draft after you completed the treatment and proposal, by capturing the basic idea and concept of the storyboards. Write it quickly, pouring your thoughts into the first draft, later drafts will allow you to make changes and add whatever you left out in this first draft. Briefly introduce characters and important action sequences, and start with a catchy teaser.

Your first draft is critical in developing the most important aspect of animation—the visual, followed with the sound of the production that includes the dialog, narration, music, and SFX. Once you complete the first acceptable draft, the voice track may be recorded. After the voice track has been recorded, individual cels or computer frames needed to cover the track may be calculated (Figure 4.7).

The Final Draft

You may need to make additional drafts as you move through the process. There will be times when you need to step away from your script and storyboards. Look carefully at your structure. Do the sequences and individual scenes or even individual shots make sense and relate what you envision follows or precedes these units? Critically, consider the length of the entire production as well as sequences. Clearly consider your characters, do they act, speak, and relate to other characters and the situation as you had planned in your original concept. Or after deep thought, if you need make some changes before you proceed.

One helpful technique is stand and read your script to several people who understand animation to listen. Watch your small audience for their reactions. Don't let others tell you what changes need to be made, but do consider their responses as objective, constructive thoughts. Corrected and final drafts follow as changes are made during the production. In some cases, an actual final script will not be written until after the postproduction stage has been completed.

Internet Problems

When you write for the Internet, you may or may not know who will be scanning your work or why they are reading it. Because the Internet is an open network (except for some private sites and networks), anyone can access your messages. For that reason, your work may be misunderstood or your carefully designed site will be hacked and destroyed or changed to say the opposite of your intent. At all times, when working on the Internet keep your vulnerability fresh in your mind. This includes the interference of spam, attachment of viruses to your work, or someone using your work for their benefit without either notifying you or paying you for your work. It is important to avoid placing any personal or revealing information of yourself on the Internet.

3:06:18   3206

THE Woods-wagon
R. Musburger
5-13-85   3-5 mins. Children's fantasy
Rev2- 6-14-85

| 1. FADE IN WS FOREST,WITH ROAD WINDING THRU TREES THE WOODS-WAGON, A STRANGE LOOKING CAR CARRYING FOUR 'CREATURES', TWO IN FRONT, TWO IN BACK. GENE IS DRIVING, PAT IS IN RIGHT FRONT, KRIS AND KIM, IN MATCHING SEMI-UNIFORMS IN BACK. | 1. SFX: WOODS, CRICKETS MUSIC: LIGHT AND BRIGHT CARTOON SFX: PUT-PUT OF FUNNY CAR |

2. MWS BUNNY RUNS IN FRONT OF WOODS-WAGON ·

2. MUSIC FADES
   SFX: BRAKES SQUEELING, MOTOR SOUNDS COUGH AND STOP

3. 2-S KRIS & KIM

3. K & K YELLING TOGETHER:
   What happened...
   KRIS: Why did we stop?
   KIM: Never mind why we stopped, just get the Woods-wagon started again..Gene and Pat...it's
   10:0 | your job to make the Woods-wagon run.

3a. CU GENE

3a.GENE: But I had to stop--you don't want me to hit the bunny
   5.73 | rabbit--do you?

3b.2-S KRIS/KIM

3b.KRIS: I don't care about any rabbit..I don't see any rabbits, and besides we're important people, the king is waiting for us to report on what those people over on the other side of the woods are going to do next.. now that we'll have shut
   15:00 | off their water.

   KIM: Hurry now, we have to get going..what are you two waiting for?
   6.7 |

Figure 4.7 First Draft

Your first draft should be as close to your concept as possible, with the understanding that several more drafts may be necessary to reach the quality of the script you want for your production. It is a starting point, but critical to your planning and thinking to complete your animation.

When you write for the Internet, you are writing for a mass medium. Sitting at your computer you may feel as if you are writing using a personal message system, but any e-mail, live chat, web page, blog, or video game may be viewed by over 100,000 strangers. Don't enter anything on the Internet that you wouldn't say to your grandmother or hand it to the first stranger you run into on the street. At the same time, the Internet may be one of the few contacts outside their immediate environment for the disabled, retired, unemployed, or some students. The Internet may also be a major factor in the lives of those who work abnormal schedules. Make certain that what you enter has value and is not a waste of your time or the time of a reader. Use your skills for positive results, not just to kill time or to massage your ego.

Writing games is more complex than the writing of any other media genre or format due to its dependence on interactivity. A quality game will offer the player a multitude of options for actions of the characters and a multitude of reactions to every action followed. Internet scripts may be created on an Excel sheet, with columns of each source for every line of action. Standard script formats of either single or dual columns, usually with the addition of at least one extra column of storyboards, are also used for games.

A flow chart showing all options and paths may also be used as a script format. An animation writer is a member of a collaborative group of people with interchangeable skills. They work as designers, artists, developers, programmers, and producers under the guidance of a publisher representing the company or studio.

Summary

This chapter concentrates on preparing you to create the final documentation needed to help you create the work you have in your mind. Some of the documentation may not be listed in the order you want or need to use on this project. But you should be aware of these documents and how to use each of them.

5

Animation Production Forms

> If you're sitting in your minivan, playing your computer animated films for your children in the back seat, is it the animation that's entertaining you as you drive and listen? No, it's the storytelling. That's why we put so much importance on story. No amount of great animation will save a bad story.
>
> **John Lasseter (2010)**

Scripts

Scripts are one of the final written formats of your production, but in reality you and your crew will make many changes as you progress through the animation process. But, the script is *your* idea, concept, and proposal now in a single written document that you will use as your key guide to your work. You need to make it specific, detailed, and as precise as you can as you move forward. There are many other script drafts you will need to consider changing, but most you will modify during the actual production process.

Script Formats

The very nature of the variety of different materials used to create animated productions demands different formats in script and storyboard layout. The script formats have been patterned after the two-column television format, the single-column dramatic film format, a modified three-column format, a specialized animation format, or even a converted multi-media script. You should use the format that best fits your production, but you should be aware of and familiar with the other formats because as your experience and career move forward, you may be required to work with whatever format is presented to you.

Two-Column Format

Because animation is more visually than aurally dependent, the two-column format allows for greater space and alignment of visuals for animated productions. The two-column format places both sound and picture elements of the script on their own spaces in the script. This makes it easier and more accurate for you as the writer and animator to isolate the portion of the script critical to each. The left-hand column lists all visuals, with camera instructions, shot framing, shot selection, and transitions all entered in capital letters.

The right-hand column lists all of the audio, including music, sound effects, and narration or dialog. All copy read by the talent is entered in upper and lowercase letters, and all other instructions are in caps. This system was developed to make it easier for talent to pick out their copy from all other instructions and for production people to concentrate on the visuals. The exception is the request by most newscaster to have their teleprompter copy entered in all bold caps (Figure 5.1).

VIDEO	AUDIO
1. SINGLE SPACE VIDEO INSTRUCTIONS	1. ANNCR: Audio copy is lined up directly across the page from its matching video.
2. TRIPLE SPACE BETWEEN EACH SHOT	2. Double space between each line of copy.
3. EACH SHOT MUST BE NUMBERED ON THE SCRIPT	3. The audio column's number must match that of its video.
4. EVERYTHING THE VIEWER IS TO SEE; ALL VISUALS, VIDEO TAPES, CG, CAMERA SHOTS, ARE INCLUDED IN THE LEFT-HAND COLUMN.	4. Everything the viewer hears; narration, music, voices, sound effects, all audio cues are in this column.
5. EVERYTHING ON THE VIDEO SIDE IS TYPED IN UPPER CASE.	5. Everything spoken by the talent is typed in upper and lower case letters. All instructions in the audio column are typed in UPPER CASE. (FADE UP NAT SOUND)
6. THE TALENT'S NAME STARTS EACH NEW LINE, BUT DOES NOT HAVE TO BE REPEATED IF THE SAME PERSON OR SOUND SOURCE CONTINUES.	6. SAM: Note—the name is in caps, what Sam says is in upper and lower case.
7. DO NOT SPLIT SHOTS AT BOTTOM OF THE PAGE.	7. Don't split words or thoughts at the end of the line or page. If the story continues to the next page, let the talent know by writing—(MORE)

Figure 5.1 Two-Column Format

The most direct and easy-to-use script format for animation is the two-column format. This format separates but keeps aligned all the audio in the right-hand column with all of the video described in the left-hand column. Whether you want to reverse which side audio or video are listed is your choice, but just be consistent for the sake of your crew and yourself.

Three-Column Format

The three-column format evolved from the two-column television and audio–visual format. The third column includes the critical storyboard frames spaced to match the visual instructions and the audio material. Such a script format expands all of the information needed to assemble the project in a concise easy-to-read format for all members of the crew and as the creator of the project, the best means of making certain the script reflects exactly what you want to create.

This format appears to be the easiest format for new comers to the field. It visually shows on one page all of the details needed to both understand what is intended for the production but also provides the critical and accurate guide for everyone involved on your production (Figure 5.2).

Single-Column Format

Most dramatic productions are shot single-camera style, and some animation and documentary writers and directors prefer the single-column script format. Since many of the writers and directors moved back and forth between shooting animation and dramatic productions, it became comfortable for some to use the same single-column format. The physical appearance of the format followed the same pattern as the film single-column format.

Film scripts became reasonably standardized in a single-column format, and animators accepted and used the single-column format depending on the studio operation and tradition. Individual portions of the script, scene description, action, movement, dialog, and the name of the actor each were set, with variations in margin depths. That made it easy for actors and crew to concentrate on their parts of the script. The format defines various aspects of the scripts by varying the width of the margins and by capitalizing certain portions of the copy.

In a full-page animation script format, a single column is devoted to both visuals and audio, which fills the entire page. The script is organized into scenes, which are numbered in a consecutive order. The location and the time of day of each scene are specified. Actions and camera movements are described in full paragraphs. Scriptwriting computer programs are available for all computer-operating systems. These programs format the script in a professional layout, relieving the scriptwriter of the tedium of worrying about margins and spacing while attempting to create a workable script (Figure 5.3).

Animation Production Forms

The creator of an animation whether producer, director, writer, animator, or animators will assume on the surface that the process is simple and straightforward. In reality, the animation production process followed by a major professional studio, a small group of animators, or a single auteur such as a student will discover that the process is complex using a computer, or using video or film as the medium.

I wrote this text for the individual regardless of the complexity of the project or the size of the group creating the animation. My advice for you to realize the documentation used in the field may be broken down into two categories: descriptions designed to explain in a narrative format what you

THREE COLUMN SCRIPT FORMAT

POISON CONTROL
Distribute to employees

30 sec.
8/23/06

VIDEO		AUDIO
1. FADE IN MS CHILD PLAYING IN FRONT OF KITCHEN CABINET		1. VO: Your home contains some of the
2. MCU FRONT OF CABINET WITH DOORS OPENING-CHILD APPROACHES. BOTTLES OF CHEMICALS MARCH OUT OF CABINET		2. half million poisons that can be
3. CU CHEMICAL-ZOOM TIGHT TO LABELS		3. disabling, if not deadly
4. XCU CROSS BONES POISON LOGO		4. MUSIC: URGENT VO: The life and well being of someone you love may depend on how quickly you reach
5. . CU HAND WRITING DOWN EMERGENCY NUMBERS		5. A Poison Control Center at these numbers: 831-6633 or 471-6026

Figure 5.2 Three-Column Format

The three-column script format combines both the traditions of the two-column format with an added third column located in the middle between the other two columns. This space allows story boards that match the audio and video columns.

5. Animation Production Forms

SINGLE-COLUMN SCRIPT FORMAT

CLIENT: Sam's Petshop   Sarah Jones

TITLE: The Doberman   2-15-13

30 Sec   Local, testimonial

---

1. INT   SAM'S PETSHOP INTERIOR LOOKING OUT TO STREET   DAY 1.

    Wild sound auto doors open/close, store nat sound as floppy-eared Doberman enters with owners at his side, owner visible from waist down only.

DOBERMAN

I may not be Lassie, but you can believe me

when I say that Sam's Pet Shop is the best

pet store in town.

2. INT   INTERIOR OF STORE, DOG & OWNER WANDERING THE AISLES   DAY 2.

    MS rear of Doberman and owner pushing shopping cart down aisle

DOBERMAN

They stock all the top brands of everything a discerning dog needs and wants.

CU large bag of dog food as it lands in cart followed by treats

DOBERMAN

Pedigree, Iams, Science Diet

Milkbones, Jerky Treats, Pig's Ears

OS Doberman looking at toys as owner reaches for rope toy

DOBERMAN

Rubber balls, squeaky toys and <u>rope</u> !!!

3. INT   STORE CHECK OUT STAND DOG & OWNER LOADED CART   DAY 3.

    Clerk checks contents of the cart, owner pays cashier reaches across counter and gives dog a treat.

4. INT   SAM'S PETSHOP LOGO   DAY 4.

DOBERMAN

Sam's Petshop – where pet's are family too.

FADE OUT

Figure 5.3 Single-Column Script

The Single-column format borrowed from theatrical script format works well for animation if the writer and director are accustomed to that style. All directions for audio and video instructions as well as some framing and transition indications appear in-line down the length of the script. Special instructions may be indicated on either the left or right margins of the script or both.

plan on doing and forms. Forms are the documentation needed to professionally organize your thoughts and actions into a logical, efficient, and sensible method of producing animation. The first four chapters of this book concentrate on the descriptive documentation of your project. This chapter and the next one give you the necessary forms needed to finish the animation you envisioned in our mind.

Time-Frame Chart

It is possible to visualize the number of frames (or timing) by marking off a frame for each 1/24th of a second if shooting in film. Computer production offers other choices depending on the system used and the technical level you wish to use. The frame rate in digital formats may vary from 30 to 60 frames per second (FPS). (Or more as new systems will keep arriving.) Calculating timing provides a means to plot out "beats" or a change in tempo to make the visual more interesting. You may use such a chart to anticipate the number of frames or visuals needed within a time period to make the point of your production or the value of the individual shot or sequence. Also, if you plan on producing an animation in stop-action, your time-frame chart will assist in your spacing of shot length.

Time charts assist you in keeping track of the amount of memory needed to complete a sequence when working in computer animation. Time-frame charts are also known as *Bounce Charts* or *Perspective Charts*, depending on the studio (Figure 5.4).

Graticule/Field Guide

A field guide is a single page, flat chart. Traditional field guides were designed to assist the animator and camera operator to align the design properly in the frame. Field guides also helped operators follow the movements designed by the animator/director. The field guide you decide to use will depend on the format you will produce and distribute, either the standard 3 × 4, a wide screen 9 × 16 format, or a square format distribution intended for cell phones or the Internet. *Layouts* were drawn maps in traditional animation to plan positioning and movement of characters and objects.

The *graticule* is a chart indicating the screen ratio of the animation. The graticule is marked off in grids to help locate exactly where objects are to be placed in the frame or what the camera or digital field is framed for each shot. Usually, graticules are no longer used in digital animation, but the philosophy of understanding how graticules may assist in accurately framing each shot should not be ignored (Figure 5.5).

Depending on the instruction you give to the computer program, based on the application you use, a field guide may indicate spatial relationships of objects in the frame or the movements of characters, duplicating the layout method for cell animation. Such programs are designed to create *motion paths* of characters or objects in each frame. Such moves are created by a "floating camera" possible using a computer equipped with such a feature. It is not possible at this time to give more specific instructions on all computer animation processes due to the rapid change in computer animation applications and new processes designed for animation production (Figure 5.6).

	S-8 mm	16 mm	35 mm	Digital
ANIMATION TIMING CHART				
Production speed (FPS)	24	24	24	30–60
Running time and shot length 1 Seconds 2 3 4	Feet+Frames 0 24 0 48 1 0 1 24	Feet+Frames 0 24 1 8 1 32 2 16	Feet+Frames 1 8 3	Frames-Frames 30 60
5 6 7 8				
9 10 11 12				
20 24 30 60				
Minutes 1 2 3 4				
5 8 10				
SUPER-8 mm **16 mm** **35 mm** **Digital**	72 Frames 40 Frames 16 Frames 30–60 Frames	Per foot Per foot Per foot Per second		

Figure 5.4 Time Chart

A time chart assists you in timing how many frames you need for each shot or sequence. It may also help to locate movements and audio synchronization. Your time chart indicates time broken down into frames plus the inches or feet if shooting film, or number of frames in either 30-frame of 60-frame digital production.

Movement Chart

Movement of any object in animation needs to consider not just the object moving in space, but how movement may affect the object. The shape of the character as it moves will change. Sometimes to show anticipation, other times to show flexibility. An object shot in space will start elongated, then when it approaches its maximum height, it will compress, come almost to a stop, and then elongate again and pick up speed as it drops. The classic example is a ball thrown into the air, falling back, reaching its logical high point, pausing falling back to ground to either bounce or roll away (Figure 5.7).

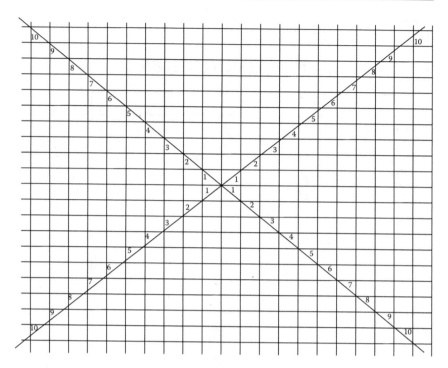

Figure 5.5 Graticule

Using a graticule chart helps orient, center, and determine locations for objects to be viewed within the frame. It may be marked off using different measurements, but the concept is based on absolute accurate placement of the guidelines.

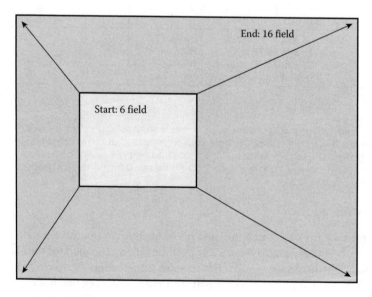

Figure 5.6 Field Guide

You use a field guide by placing it over (digitally or visually) a graticule for precise placement of objects in your shot. I may be used to plan moves, or changing in framing.

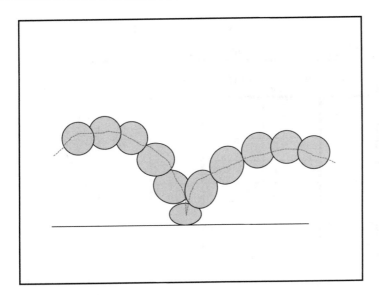

Figure 5.7 Movement Chart

Movement charts will assist you in determining if you need to modify the shape of a character or object as it moves through your frame. It also should guide you in calculating how to locate an object as it moves through space.

Dope Sheet

A *Dope Sheet* may also be called an X-sheet or exposure sheet. Despite the arrival of computers in animation, some of the traditional forms used for years still find a place to assist in moving your animation process forward efficiently and accurately. Your easily drawn and filled in dope sheet may be drawn on an (XLR) sheet or other lined format application. This method lays out all of the necessary details in an orderly manner making it easy to find the information quickly when needed. A dope sheet provides the critical information not only for you but also for everyone else on your team.

Generally, the information you should include on your dope sheet would be: sequence number, scene number, scene start and end points, shooting/scanning instructions, and instructions for layers, listed in chronological order, leaving spaces for notes, comments, and after-thoughts (Figure 5.8).

Cel List/Frame List/Shooting Sheet/Exposure Sheet

In cel production, the outline of the character or object is drawn in black on the front of the individual cel, and then painters will add the color on the backside of the cels, frame by frame. A parallel process occurs in digital animation by assembling individual scene files into a final and permanent form. Notes on movement, color, and transitions are included on a cel or frame list with each frame. Each space is labeled a color, and that space will carry that assigned color in each frame wherever that shape appears. In 3-D, texture mapping creates solid surfaces and surface textures.

Each of these same stages is followed if the production uses dimensional materials such as sand, clay, or paper cutouts instead of cels or a digital program.

EXPOSURE (Dope) SHEET

TITLE _____ SCENE _____ ANIMATOR _____ SHEET# _____

FRAME	ACTION	SETTING	LAYERS					CAMERA
			4	3	2	1	BG	

Figure 5.8 Dope Sheet

A traditional animation production form used to accurately plot each item scheduled to appear in each frame. Dope sheets may also be called: exposure sheet, frame list, cell list, or shooting sheet.

The difference is that each frame is a physical set-up. Once the characters and objects are arranged on a dimensional set, they must be lit. Then, the camera operator shoots individual frames before moving each character or object and shooting the next exposure.

Exposure sheets provide another method to keep accurate track of what each frame should contain, the length to hold on each frame, and any camera movements and transitions you want to include in your special effects. You may add any additional items such as shot number, file number, sequence and scene numbers, or any detail you need to keep in mind while working on that scene or sequence that you don't want to forget. This type of diagram will help you stay focused and prevent you from becoming lost in the complexities of your project (Figure 5.9).

Backgrounds and Key Frames

Backgrounds provide a setting or environment for your story. In cel animation, the background is a separate cel or series of cels; in digital animation, the background may be a single or series of specific files showing the setting of the scene or sequence. Backgrounds in traditional animation were separate drawings from the foreground characters. You may move the background between each

EXPOSURE SHEET

SCENE	TITLE	ANIMATOR	FOOTAGE	TEST NUMBER
			TIME	

ACTION	#	4	3	2	1	BXGD	#	CAMERA
	1							
	2							
	3							
	4							
	5							
	6							
	7							
	8							
	9							
	0							
	1							
	2							
	3							
	4							
	5							
	6							
	7							
	8							
	9							
	0							

Figure 5.9 Shooting Sheet/Cell/Frame List/Exposure Sheet

All of the forms labeled exposure sheet, dope sheet, cell list, frame list, and shooting sheet may be similar or essentially the same, depending on individual studio or director's preference. The form may be deigned horizontally or vertically as long as all of the necessary information is included in format that serves the purpose of the form.

exposure of each frame. In digital animation, you may program the move as you decide to match the action of the characters in the foreground. Each move may be programmed separately.

Key frames show an object or character in a specific position such as showing a start, end, or key movement position of the object in your scene. In most cases, you will have created at least two key frames to show a complete action. When you are ready, you will fill in the frames by using the "Inbetween" process of adding the movements between your key frames. Key frames may be used as a "hold" to draw attention to the specific position of a character. You may modify the key frame by adding small changes in the hold sequence, often back and forth between the hold and another repeated frame. You may also use key frames to save time when animating the character running,

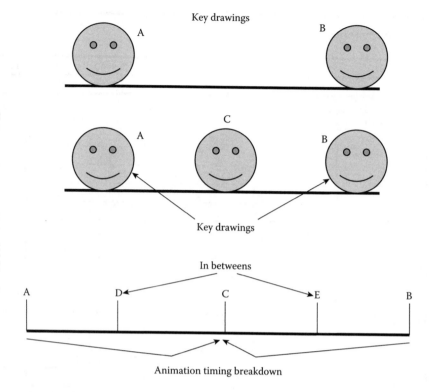

Key drawings

Key drawings

In betweens

Animation timing breakdown

Figure 5.10 Key Frames

A key frame chart is designed to assist you in planning placement of objects in the frame. This process becomes more difficult if you are recording a series that requires calculating positioning of inbetween images once the key images have been located in space.

walking, or moving in a set direction or pattern. Typically, the sixth frame of a running scene will be the key frame, repeated as you need to set the speed and action (Figure 5.10).

Program/Production/Progress Charts

Animation production is a team process, even if you are writing, producing, animating, and directing your own short. The process of maintaining an efficient and creative flow means everyone involved must be kept informed and up-to-date on each step of them process. This includes you keeping all of the processes of your production organized and in order. Individuals or studios may use different forms, depending on their personal preferences and the size and complexity of their production.

Two aspects are important. First, you need to keep accurate track of the progress of the project. Know exactly where you are in the step-by-step system of creating and organizing each aspect of your project. Second, be aware of which aspect needs to be accomplished in which order to avoid wasting time and energy by incorrectly completing one task before the task that should be finished first you have not yet started. *Project* or *Progress Charts* may give you the way to keep organized.

PROGRAM CHART
CLIENT
PRODUCTION
SERIES

Seq	Br	Fr	Description	Story	Lay	Ani	Clean	Col	Ef	Comp	Cast	Rec	Comments
1	A	90	WS Open Titles										
2	A	10											
3	C	35											
4	C	60											
5	B	78											
6	D	3											
7	E	45											
8	F	35											
9	A	75											
10	A	10											
11	B	5											
12	B	22											
13	E	85											
14	F	33											
15	D	50											
16	D	25											
17	A	34											
18	A	15											
19	B	20											
20	B	10											

Figure 5.11 Program Chart

Program, production, and progress charts assist you in careful planning and then controlling the production process as it moves forward. A variety of labels and specific format designs for such forms will appear within the industry at the desires or policies of individual studies or directors.

The complexity of your project may require you to work out on a day-by-day schedule, listing each step that needs to be finished by a certain day or group of days. The idea of managing your creative idea could seem to be counterproductive. But, regardless of the size of a project, there has to be some sort of log to keep track of what needs to be accomplished, as well as what has been accomplished. Another critical aspect of scheduling keeps track of team members fulfilling their responsibilities on schedule. Most importantly, the value that should not be wasted is *time*: your time, your school's time, your producer's time, and/or the funding sources time. Completion schedules must be kept and met. Keeping completion schedules is a golden rule of the animation business, as well as all creative businesses (Figure 5.11).

Route Sheets

The route sheet is a detailed record of all materials and personnel responsible for each operation of the project. Another method of keeping track of every step of your project is to create a *Route Sheet*. This sheet may be created on a spreadsheet with each sequence listed on the left-hand column, and the stages of the project are the headings for the columns. This type of record is helpful, if not a necessity, if you are using several crew members, each working on different aspects of your project. As each step is completed, or when each step has reached a completion, that fact is marked on the chart.

A major use for the *Route Sheet* is when a project will be completed at a location separate from the originating studio or artist. (An assistant known as a checker's assistant is responsible to make certain that all parts of the media

Seq	Fr	Description	Story	Lay	Ani	Clean	Col	Ef	Comp	Cast	Rec	Comments
1	90											
2	10											
3	35											
4	60											
5	78											
6	3											
7	45											
8	35											
9	75											
10	10											
11	5											
12	22											
13	85											
14	33											
15	50											
16	25											
17	34											
18	15											
19	20											
20	10											

ROUTE SHEET
CLIENT
PRODUCTION
SERIES — COMPLETION DATE/TIME

Figure 5.12 Route Sheet

Some forms used in animation production may be assigned a range of different uses and purposes. Route sheets may be drawn to provide specific means of keeping a project on schedule. The same form may also be used for moving parts of an animation production from one location to another.

being shipped are properly included, packed, labeled, and returned on schedule.) For you, a route sheet becomes one of the best methods of knowing exactly how each step of your project has progressed toward your goal of a completed project (Figure 5.12).

Color Assignments

Soon after deciding on the critical aspects of your animation project, you should start to decide on how you will use color. Color defines many portions of your story. The setting, the time of day, whether it is a serious, comical, or documentary, may be defined by the colors used. Color has psychological values because humans react to colors differently depending on culture and environment. Colors also affect space perception. Warm red colors appear to move closer. Cool blue colors appear to recede. These matters are very specific not only in the colors of the character's costumes and faces, but also the props and settings.

You must consider carefully the relationship of the foreground object's color and the colors used to depict the background. Obviously, some form of contrast will be needed, but you should not distract your audience's interest in your characters dialog or actions with a background that side-tracks your story. Each character or object in your story needs to have a specific color model or sheet showing what each part of the character's costume, body part, and/or object in the scene will be colored. In cel animation, the person responsible for the color of all objects is labeled the inker or painter. Each cel and background sheet are painted and photographed separately. In digital production, the person responsible for

COLOR ASSIGNMENTS	
BACKGROUNDS	Occupies 90% of each scene, despite being static The key to the mode, mood, and emotion Avoid distracting from foreground action/characters Avoid fine texture, watercolor one of best media
COLOR KEY	Create a color board or palette as guide Key portion of character model sheet Determine character colors starting with featured performers and then move to supporting roles Skin, hair, mouth, costume
COLOR STYLING	Props, scene settings, effects Design differences between day, night, weather Think carefully of texture and effects of lighting Make a judgment on color variations of hue, contrast, tint, density, saturation, and reflection. Consider audience response from culture, age, gender
COLOR PSYCHOLOGY	Depends on culture, experience, mental factors Warm colors: red, orange indicate movement—forward Cool colors: blues, greens indicate stability—withdraw

Figure 5.13 Color Assignment

Since color carries a variety of values in an animation production in setting the mode or the mood of the production, it also affects the audience's reaction to cultural and psychological responses to specific colors. You must consider carefully each color in your production.

the same function is called a colorist. In both 2-D and 3-D digital animation, the images are composed in a process called compositing. The digital process is much faster, easier to make changes, and avoids problems of layers of cells causing a change in the tone of colors painted within different levels of cels. In 3-D animation, you must take into consideration the texture of the surface of all objects including characters. The surface of each object may be depicted as having different textures than you would be able to show in any 2-D animation (Figure 5.13).

Summary

The forms described in this chapter range from script format choices to charts calculating timing, scheduling, movements, placement within the frame, and a section on color assignments. Each of these charts (sheets forms) are useful to an individual animator or a large-scale animation studio regardless of the complexity of the animation production.

6

Final Production: Audio and Postproduction

Audio-Sound Production
Sound Tracks
Recording Techniques
Lip Sync
Mouth Shapes

Final Production Process Stage
Production Schedule
Production Folders
Postproduction
Summary

... not only is animation a form of film, —animation is not only an art. And it is not only the life and motion of a genre of film, of cinema, of film 'as such'. It is far more. It is idea, concept, process, performance, medium and milieu; and it invests all arts, media and communications. It invests all sciences and technologies. It invests all disciplines, knowledges, fields, practices (including the history of ideas, the history of philosophy).

Alan Cholodenko (2015)

This chapter covers the final stages of your production. This chapter starts with the sound or audio and winds up with a listing of the methods you use to finally wrap your animation and prepare to enjoy the fruits of your labors. There actually are no final chapters in the field of animation. Each hour of each day, new technologies are being tried, developed, and handed over to all of you producers to make something new and wonderful using your mind and your skills.

Audio-Sound Production

The difference between sound and audio may be a semantic difference between technologists and audiologists. For some, sound is what we hear, whereas audio is the technical description of electronics that create an audible response in a human or other creatures. Regardless of solving this question in this text, sound and audio will mean the same unless there is a specific technical reason to differentiate the two terms.

Research has shown that from 60% to 70% of the response to an animation story comes from the audio rather than the visual. This is important despite animation's power of using visuals to tell a story. You may be faced with the problem of deciding whether to start the development of your concept with the audio or the visual. Generally, for the beginner, starting with the visual produces a better result. If you would rather start with sound, then your first assignment is to create a *Sound Treatment*. This is a detailed listing of the timing of all sounds beginning with narration or dialog, then effects, followed by music. If there is unusual use of music used as effects, or music is the key to timing, pace, and rhythm of the production, then that should be dealt with at the end. Sound effects are usually added in the end unless those sounds are critical to the story itself. After carefully calculating how many frames of sound and for how long each sound will last, you can design the visual to match each sound segments.

In all media productions, there are three basic sounds: voice, effects, and music. How much of each of the three you use and how they relate will be the basis of your audio plan. Voice includes dialog and narration. Dialog is the conversation spoken between characters and the speaking patterns of your characters, both from individuals as well as how the characters relate and speak back and forth. Narrations are voices from off-camera. Using narration avoids having to design a specific visual character and avoiding lip sync during that character's speeches. Voices reveal a character's background and culture through the accent, phrasing, and other speech patterns.

Music provides the soul, mood, and a method of setting emotional aspects of your production that may be difficult to easily visualize. Music, like animation, is a mathematical system which depends on regular patterns of rhythms and beats. You may use various tempos of jazz, country, rap, or other popular types of music to set a scene, locate an environment, or establish the attitude of the characters. You could start with a recorded piece of music and then create an animation to that music. Be aware of and fully confident of who owns the rights to any recorded music. That does not mean just the performer. Writers, publishers, and distributors all may have rights that need to be met. Best use your own recording of your own music to avoid such complex legal problems.

Effects should match specific sounds: a gunshot, dropping water, door slam, anything you can think of sounds around you that you might forget are there. Use those sounds, but keep in mind actual sounds may not match what is depicted in your animated figure. A car crash may not really sound authentic in an animated situation. Each effect must be considered, tested, and corrected to make it work for the desired reaction from the audience.

You may find that in today's easily produced Internet and blog animation, the tendency is to depend on dialog rather than visual action. It is cheaper to let the characters tell the story rather than to show the action. Creating visuals requires more time and effort raising costs rather than writing dialog. Music, sound effects, voiceover narration, and dialog without lip synchronization describe the story, rather than acting out the action to show the audience the story. But relying primarily on sound to tell the story limits the power of visuals. If you are going to tell your story using animation, then you had better learn to concentrate on visuals and reinforce visuals with the audio.

Your critical decisions between visuals and audio may depend on finances and time available to produce your concept. But finally you have to decide what will best tell your story with the time and facilities available to you. Think carefully, what carries the greater power, the pictures or the sounds you create.

Sound Tracks

Once your concept has been fleshed out and a complete script written, then production may begin. You must record the sound track first. Once recorded, you carefully analyze and time, word-by-word your track. You need to record this analysis on a form that you understand and provides you useful means for keeping track of each of the sounds and timing in your production. Such a form may be labeled: dope sheet, bar chart/sheet, dialog test sheet, and exposure sheet.

Dope Sheet/Bar Chart/Bar Sheet/Dialog
Test Sheet/Exposure Sheet

Each studio operation designs its own chart, regardless of what they call it, but there is a pattern that can be used in any situation. The chart may be laid out using an application like Microsoft Excel or Apple's Numbers. The sheet may appear to be complicated but the concept is to organize each aspect of your animation so that you know exactly where you are as you shoot or record each frame.

Your sheet, regardless of what you call it, lists each frame to be created, along with the three accompanying tracks: dialog, music, and sound effects (SFX). The sheet consists of a chart based on scenes broken down into increments of 1/24th or 1/30th of a second. Film is exposed at the rate of 24 FPS, and digital recordings are normally exposed at 30 or 60 FPS. Most animation uses exposures of 2 or 3 frames per cel, rather than one cel for each frame. This reduces the number of cels needed without decreasing the flow of the visual.

You need to decide how to arrange your columns and sections. One system uses the horizontal lines to list each frame of the animation. The number of FPS/minute for film, video, and digital each may be different, but the idea is to allow for a space to describe each and every frame individually or in sequences. In this system, the vertical columns may be broken down in a variety of different ways, but a starting point could be: first column, a section for notes that may cover the action in more than one frame; second column lists the dialog, phonetically frame by frame. An additional column could list music or sound effects in the same manner. Several more columns may be needed to list different levels of animation added to each individual frame if the project uses layers of animation for each frame or sections of frames. The final column of this section should be a designator for the background and how long that background will be used until the next one starts. The final and widest column is intended to allow space for more notes, specifically for the camera operator to indicate transitions, special visual effects, panning, and other shot instructions.

If accurately laid out, it is possible at a glance to see what happens in each second and minute of the production. At the top of each sheet, the sequence and scene numbers need a slot, as well as the name of the production and a sheet number, since even a short animation will require many sheets. The same form used as a dope sheet works well as a dialog test sheet. One additional column might break the dialog down into two parts: the actual spoken words and a parallel column showing a phonetic breakdown.

A crew person known as a *track reader* listens carefully to the audio track frame by frame. Then, the recorded words are transposed to the words phonetically

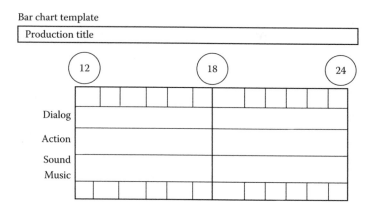

Bar chart template

Figure 6.1 Bar Sheet/Chart

You may keep accurate track of exactly how you want all of the sounds that make up the audio portion of your production by using some form of a bar chart that indicates by specific frame location each sound.

equivalent of each word frame by frame. This provides a detailed account of how the individual words both actually and phonetically fit the individual frames and series of frames. If you are producing on film, the task is easy since you can see each frame and match the audio to it. On video or a digital production, you may need to use a stop watch or the Time Line on the computer to give you an accurate idea where the voice needs to fit the visual. You could use the application Flash to watch a waveform of the voice and/or music to select changes in individual frames and maximize timing.

These charts may be drawn using a horizontal layout. The vertical columns now are the individual frames, and the horizontal rows may be used to enter dialog, phonetized dialog, action, music, sound effects, or other notes. Each page needs to be identified by the name of your production, sequence, and scene. The individual frames are marked, and then by counting the number of frames in a second/minute, additional marks are placed to indicate the time factors.

All these forms may be duplicated using a computer applications such as Premiere, Flash, Director, After Effects, Pro Tools, GarageBand, and other applications (Figure 6.1).

Recording Techniques

You may choose several different methods of recording your production soundtrack. You may record using an analog or digital tape deck, either reel-to-reel or cassette. If shooting straight to film, you may want to record on a multitrack analog or digital tape deck and then convert each track to a separate film track. You could record directly onto your computer using a flexible audio-recording application such as GarageBand, Pro Tools, Flash, QuickTime Pro, or Premiere. These same applications also are handy to complete your editing before you animate to match the soundtrack.

Recording voices should be accomplished in a soundproof area separate from the actual recording equipment. This provides a "clean" signal without any interference from the external noise of recorders, other equipment, or people. As the director, you tell the actor whatever you want. A reasonable actor will respond to

RECORDING TECHNIQUES

Recording Media
    Analog tape deck
    Multi-track analog tape deck
    Digital tape deck
    Analog cassette deck
    Direct to computer
        GarageBand, ProTools, Flash, Quicktime Pro, Premiere
    Dub to film track recorder

Recording techniques
    Soundproof enclosure, separate record room
    Director–actor relationship
    Record continuous take
    Video record actor for facial expressions

Music—Sound effects recording
    Same as voice technique
    Effects in short takes for ease in editing
    Clear rights for all pre recorded music
    Record self-created music

Figure 6.2 Chart of Recording Techniques

Recording your audio track may be accomplished on either a digital format, using any of several computer apps, or digital or analog recording techniques on tape decks. The key to quality recording is to approach the process with care and understanding of how important accurate sound is to your production.

your directions on the tempo, where to emphasis a word or phrase. Try to record each take in a continuous pass. This helps the actor maintain character and the feeling what they are trying to transmit with their voice. Allow actors to physically react to their lines, Your actors may make faces, move around, and show emphasis with their bodies. If you record them on video, you will find it helpful to pattern your drawn character to the actor's actions.

Recording yourself or other musicians should be accomplished in the same soundproof area and with as much care as you used to record your voice track. It is much easier to work with a "clean" soundtrack than one that has to be cleaned-up to remove unwanted sounds or unnecessary noise. Sound effects may be recorded as you recorded voice, but in small pieces or sections that allow you to edit whatever effect you need into the length, loudness, and feeling for that segment of your production (Figure 6.2).

Lip Sync

One of the most difficult animation techniques, regardless of the medium, is creating and maintaining *start by* between the sounds, especially voices and the movement of the character on screen. This process is called maintaining *lip sync*. Each set of vowels and consonants requires a different shape of the mouth for realistic action. The changes of the shapes must match the voice on the track. Timing is the key to lip sync and combining voices, sound effects, and music to appear and be heard at exactly the correct relative time. Consider your production as a series of frames, whether you are producing on film, videotape, recording on digital media, or directly using a computer. Even though there might not be a specific frame in a computer file, the time on computers may be broken down in whatever the system timing factor has been set.

Lip sync starts with a detailed analysis of all dialog in your production. Be aware! Sometimes sync is not always necessary. Looking at something and not actually seeing the same object is much like listening and not really hearing the correct sound. Information from a character's voice is important, but no more so than the motion, position, and changes in the character's body. Lip sync starts with a detailed analysis of all dialog in your production.

Once you know what is important in your character's expression that requires a synced lip motion, then you should proceed to your analysis. At times, you need to sync only the words that are important to the specific statement, not every word. Start by creating a phonetic breakdown. Record the sound, then analyze frame by frame which specific sound appears at which frame and for how long. Each character's words, sounds, and music if specific to the point need to be carefully calibrated and entered on a bar chart explained in the next section.

A basic technique of matching facial expressions with sounds is for you to record your script (slowly) with a camera close on your face. You can pull single frames of your face and print them as a means of studying the actual shape of the mouth, eyebrow, nose, and other facial features. Also, you may watch the changes in your face as the mouth moves from one part of a word to another. You should create mini-guides for specific character's faces and expressions. Character's mouth movements are shown in the next section under "Mouth Shapes."

An additional form of synchronization is called counterpointing. That effect is created by a mismatch between the actual sound and the visual that matches it. Anticipating or delaying a sound may strengthen the effect or add a comical effect. For maximum effect, especially for comedy, you should record a loud or sudden sound at least 6–10 frames ahead of the actual visual. This warns and prepares the audience for the effect (Figure 6.3).

Mouth Shapes

All speech, therefore mouth shapes, is based on phonetics. Phonetics is a study of the vocal sounds based on changes in the mouth, throat, and lips to create a specific sound, regardless of the actual spelling or pronunciation of that word. The shape of a mouth when speaking vowel sounds is more important than the shape of a mouth when speaking consonants. The vowel sounds, a, e, i, o, u, usually require opening the mouth and changing the position of mouth and tongue to make the vowel sounds. Most consonant sounds can be shown as nearly fixed thin-line of the lips.

The character's personality and actions will depend on what the animated character is saying. Mouth shapes need to be dawn with other features of a face as well as the lips. A smile is different than a frown, but the mouth may be the same. The eye shape and form may change as well as the position of the nose, and wrinkles change with different sounds including laughter.

Column1	Column	Column	Column	Colum	Column	Column7	
Sequence	Scene		Actor				Sheet
		3	2	1	BG	CAMERA	
	////		1				
	+		3			*START*	
	∞ο		5				
			7				
	B		9				
	EE		11				
			13				
	O R		15				
			17				
	N		19				
	O		21				
	T		23				
	+		25				
	OO		27				
	B		29				
	EE		31				
	////		33				
	////		35			Cut	

LIP SYNC

Figure 6.3 Lip Sync Chart

Since facial expressions are so important in animation, accurately synchronized sound with facial and mouth position is critical. Each section where the face of a character is clearly visible needs to analyzed to determine what shape the mouth needs to be within each frame.

You should draw a face/mouth chart for each character. Different mouth shapes for each expression, including the eyes, nose, and other parts of the face for each character, make up the heart of the face/mouth chart. This needs to be a fairly detailed and comprehensive chart so that you will not change a character's personality by forgetting how you want it to look in different speaking situations. You may use body movements to reinforce sounds by synchronizing or exaggerating the moment with a swing of the arms, forward or backward motion of the entire body.

When trying to match mouth shapes with the sounds a character makes, it is not necessary to use a mouth shape for every letter of a word spoken. Depending on the accent or speech pattern, often the sound of "L" is omitted. Carefully watch yourself in a mirror as you speak the lines, or record your actor speaking the lines to determine which mouth shapes are actually needed for each frame.

To learn how and where to place various mouth shapes to match the lip sync variations requires the creation of a "Dope Sheet," "Bar Sheet," "Dialog Test Sheet," or a printout of a file from a computer sound application. On this sheet, each sound, not necessarily which letter of the word, is marked where that sound falls in relationship to the rest of the sounds of the word that may precede or following that sound (Figure 6.4).

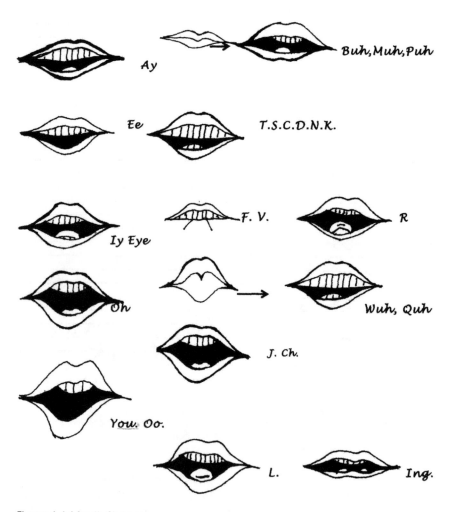

Figure 6.4 Mouth Shapes

One of the best methods of reaching an understanding of how to depict character's facial expressions determined by the shape of the mouth in an animation project is to watch yourself in a mirror as you speak the lines. A study of phonetics will help you reach that understanding.

Final Production Process Stage

The Final Production Process Stage varies depending on the length of your production, the type of animation used, the size of the studio, and the budget. The independent animator today may raise the funds needed, write the script, draw the cels or use a computer program, assemble the story, and prepare it for distribution entirely on their own as an auteur. But, if all of the work is accomplished by one person, the final production process follows a reasonably parallel path regardless of whether the animation production is the simplest or the most complex.

Production Schedule

Creating an efficient and logical production schedule is the first step in your final production process. Thinking about formally organizing your creative process seems like a contradiction. But, it is not a contradiction. Actually, the more you carefully preorganize your thought processes, as well as your plan for the actual production of your animation, the easier, more efficient, less time-consuming, and less expensive your production process will be.

A formal plan drawn out in a chart of some type will provide the basis and stability of your project. The chart may be as simple as a list of the steps you intend on taking with approximate time indications when each step will be completed. This chart may also be designed to list each sequence or scene of your animation and the order you plan on creating them. The schedule could also indicate the importance of each step and who is responsible for its completion.

Instead of a chart of columns and rows, the schedule could be drawn as a flowchart. You will indicate each stage of the production by name with either references to time factors, or at least the order of progress. Specific dates and crew assignments may be included (Figure 6.5).

Production Folders

A production folder will provide a final resting place for all notes, documents, and other information concerning each aspect of your animation. Ideally, the folder will be a series of internal folders. You will need to create one folder for each scene, sequence, or even each shot of your animation. Then, the master folder will become a file by file of every detail of your production. A folder may consist of individual cards or pages or computer files of each part of your production. It then provides a detailed means of reviewing and/or recording every aspect of what you have spent so much time working on. This file of folders will not only save the documentation of your work but also become the means of reminding you all of the good and poor memories of the production (Figure 6.6).

Postproduction

The postproduction stage of your film animation may consist of simply printing a copy of the edited film combined with a mix of the sound tracks or a frame-by-frame recording, adding visual effects, and rearranging shots to remove

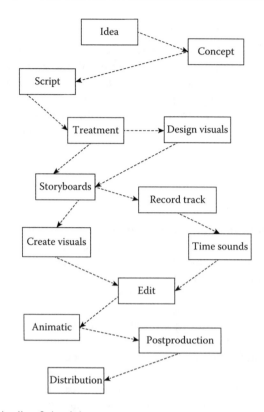

Figure 6.5 Production Schedule

Production schedules may take a variety of different forms, including adapting other scheduling forms you have already designed for your project. But, it is important to keep in mind the concept of following a process that does not leave out any critical aspect of your production.

unwanted images, such as power lines, or unwanted sounds. The final stage for your digital-animated production involves *rendering* the original virtual files into a conformed final file that may be duplicated or converted to film or videotape or a digital medium for distribution.

Each step of your final postproduction should consist of at least two, if not three different final copies. The first is called a *Line Test*. You use this copy to double check every aspect of your production to make certain it meets your plan and idea. If changes need to be made, then make them now, because any changes requested later may become very expensive and unnecessarily time consuming to complete to meet your standards.

The last two copies are called the *Final Copy* and/or the *Answer Copy*.

Either or both of them may also be called the Final Print or the Answer Print, terms left over from the days of film production. This last stage is made after making certain every aspect of your production is correct and ready to be distributed. That's why the last final copy/print is the Answer Print.

NEW ANIMATION					
Sc#	Seq.#	BG	Animator	Camera	Fr#
COMMENTS					

This folder or file may be created as a hard form—a series of file cards to be sorted and filed in a container for ready access.

OR

This folder can be a guide for creating individual digital records of each aspect of your production. Then, the individual entries may be combined into a folder on your computer for ready access.

Figure 6.6 Production Folder

To provide yourself a reminder and an accurate record of what you have accomplished, you ought to maintain a file of production folders. Each folder describes each segment, whether it is a scene, a sequence, or even a single shot. These folders provide the final documentation of your project.

Summary

The last chapter of this book is like the last scene of your animation. It needs to be concise, to the point, and leave the reader with a full feeling of having accomplished something by participating in the project. Unfortunately, it is not possible to include every aspect of animation production in one text. You should, at this point, review in your mind what you have learned, what you still need to learn, and how you may improve your animation production skills. Then, finish your project, review it carefully, show it to a discerning and appreciative audience, listen to their thoughts and comments, take notes, and then fill in the blanks by reading and watching more animation.

After that start working on your next *idea*.

Glossary

ABOVE-THE-LINE: Both the expenses and category of administration personnel of most media production units.

ADR (Automatic Dialog Replacement): Dialog added to a production to reach synchronization or to replace poor quality or incomplete audio.

AMBIENT SOUNDS: Background sounds or sounds existing in a location, not directly related to the production.

ANIMATIC: A film or digital storyboard created by combining a series of digital files of each frame or sequence or a film series of preparatory animation frames prepared as a test of a story and to test timing of the production.

ANIME: Animation developed in Japan, produced primarily for a youth market.

ANSWER PRINT: The first literal print copy of a production as a trial or test copy before accepting the production as final and ready to be released.

ANTAGONIST: In a story, one of two characters who represent the conflict of the story. The antagonist usually is a negative character or is cast to oppose the protagonist.

ANTICIPATION: Anticipation is the first of three stages in animation movement. It gives the viewer an advanced notice of a coming movement, an action often in a negative direction to the following action.

ARTIFACT: Any part of an image or sound clip left over from the encoding/transcoding process, which may be caused by unknown interference or analog noise.

AUDIO: The sound portion of a media production, narration, music, SFX, character speech.

AUDIO–VISUAL: A combination of visual material accompanied with corresponding sound distributed via videotape, film, slides, computer projection, or any means of displaying the material.

AURAL: Referring to sound, or voicing of a character.

AUTEUR: A term referring to a media creator who performs the function of all major creative crew members. One person serving as writer, producer, and director.

AUTHOR: Often used to refer to the person converting audio, video, graphics into a standard format.

BATCH: A group of files or frames that may be handled simultaneously.

BEATS: Assembling a group of similar items such as video or audio clips in a production. Such a batch could be modified simultaneously instead of having to do the changes individually on each item. Also, one method of braking down the movements in a program to anticipate pace and rate.

BLOCK: A group of pixel elements in a defined matrix within the video frame. A block may be handled as a single item for encoding or other changes.

BLOG: A website updated regularly on a specific topic usually by one person.

BOOTLEG: To copy, or distribute someone else's creative material without the copywrite owner's permission or without paying the proper licensing fee.

BRAINSTORMING: A session of writers suggesting, discussing, editing, and arguing over scripts, creative and production ideas.

CAUCASIAN: An anthropological classification of people by racial heredity, from Europe, North Africa, and Southwest Asia, in some case also classified as "white".

CGI (Computer-generated Imagery): An application used to create graphic images for any digital system, art, photography, cinema, and TV.

CEL (or Cell): In traditional animation, plastic sheets, often cellulose acetate, were used to draw the outline of each frame of the animation. Once the cell outline is completed, the colors were added on the reverse side before going before the camera for recording.

CHARACTER DEVELOPMENT: Each character in an animation must have a distinct personality, movement, and appearance that fits the plot and action needed to move the story and relationship forward.

CHARGE-BACK: An accounting system of calculating where each cost of an animation should be allotted to.

COLLAGE: An artwork usually consisting of a variety of different images and different types of images superimposed or arranged in abstract patterns.

COMPOSITING: The process of combining all of the visual aspects of a frame into one complete unit, either physically or digitally.

CONSONANTS: The close-mouthed letters of the alphabet: B, C, D, F, G, H, J, K, L, M, N, P, Q, R, S, T, V, W, X, Y, and Z.

CONTRADICTION: An item created in the opposite of another item.

COPYRIGHT: A legal right documented by the Federal Government indicating the right of ownership and control over any form of expression: production or document, including all forms of music.

COUNTERPOINTING: In audio, using sounds in opposition to another sound.

CROSSOVER: Editing a scene by showing different actions alternating even though they occur simultaneously.

DESIGNATOR: Usually, a specific name of a locator or person making a decision.

DETRIMENT: A negative reaction or action.

DIALOG: Words spoken by a character, usually on camera, if not, then it becomes narration.

DOCUMENTATION: Generally, any record, but more specifically usually the written (or digital record) of information.

DRAFT(S): Each version of a script is a draft, indicating that the script is in the process of being developed with possible changes as the process continues.

DRAMATIC STRUCTURE: Traditionally, dramatic structure is built on three levels of dramatic action. The first is exposition, explaining what the story is about and introducing the characters; the second is building action and leading to the major conflict; the third is the conflict comes to a crisis, is resolved, and the story ends, happily, or not.

DYNAMIC: Active movement of a story, characters, or other objects in a story.

EFX (Effects): Usually referred to as visual effects, rain, explosion, digital modulation.

ELONGATED: An object has been stretched out in one direction.

ETHNICITY: A sociological ranking of ethnic believes or cultural traditions.

EXPLICIT: Meaning a price's description.

EXTERIOR: The outer surface of a building or location.

EXTERNAL: Located outside.

FCC (Federal Communications Commission): United States government agency responsible for setting the rules and regulations of broadcasting, cable, telephony, satellite, and other communication media.

FILTER: The material placed in front of a lens to modify the image or in video, any aspect of electronics may be modified such as exposure, saturation, resolution, or special effects.

FIRSTPLAY: The first signal viewed on a DVD or other disc when first played. Usually, a test signal of logo of the producer.

FLEXIBILITY: Being able to vary in position, size, and shape of an object.

FLIPBOOK: A collection of single animation frames designed to be handheld and create movement by releasing each page in quick succession. Also, a digital app to accomplish the same view.

FLOW CHART: A method of organizing all the material, actions, and processes of an animation project to assist in keeping the process organized and on schedule.

FLY-BY: A term used to describe shooting a visual from the air via an airplane, helicopter, or drone.

FOLDER: A digital carrier designed to hold more than one individual file.

FOUND OBJECTS: Any unique item salvaged from the trash or any other throw-away source.

GAG (GAG Meeting): A meeting of writers working on jokes and humorous aspects of an animation production.

GARBAGE MATTE: A preliminary matte used to isolate parts of an image to be modified separately from the rest of the images.

GENDER: Classification of a person's sexual identity.

GENRE: The definition of the style of a media production: Western, Mystery, Sci-Fi, and Fantasy.

HEADER: A system of identifying a file, whether it is a GOP (Group of Pictures), MPEG files, or other sequences of information that need to be easily identified.

HORIZONTAL: A line, object, or part of a scene that lies parallel to the horizon. In charts, the lines that run from left to right, or vice versa, but always parallel to the horizon.

HUMANIZE: To modify a nonhuman figure, animal, or object into an object that resembles or acts like a human.

INDENT: To insert space to the borders of the margin.

INTERACTIVE: A media controlled by the audience using a keyboard. Mouse or some other digital interface.

INTERIOR: The inside of a building, room, or other location of a production.

INTERNAL: Inside an object or space.

INTERSTICES (McClaren): The invisible but still present factors that make animation as fascinating and mysterious as it is.

IPOD: A portable media player manufactured by Apple.

"ISMS": A syllable added to a word to change its meaning … usually to the opposite.

KEY FRAMES: A single frame showing a character of an object in a static position to help determine how the next frames should be created to carry the movement on as planned.

LAYOUTS: A drawing created for a scene, showing the background, critical characters, positions, and possible moves.

LEICA REEL: see Animatic.

LINE TEST: A series of animation drawings copied in order on a digital or film format in order so that the series may be projected to check the quality and timing of the production.

LIP SYNC: The matching of the movement of the mouth of a character to the matching sound, or the matching of the visual sound to an action or visual effects.

LITANY: A supplication or invocations by a leader expecting a response.

MASK: To modify a portion of the alpha channel's transparency. In After Effects, if may define a path of a text file.

MODEL SHEET: Each character or an object in an animation needs a chart showing as many different poses and angles of view for reference. Critical to include proportions of each character or object.

MOTIONPATHS: A chart or series of drawings, indicating the directions and movements of characters within a frame.

MOTIVATION: The reasons characters act, speak, and react to each action in an animation.

MULTIMEDIA: A production utilizing more than one media.

MUSIC RIGHTS: The legal description of the control the originator of an artistic object or publication, including music, has over the use, duplication, and sale of that item

NARRATION: The off-camera voice of the character or talent.

NATIVE: The original chip format from a source such as a camera.

NONLINEAR: The process of editing out of order, any portion of the project may be edited before the rest of the project since all of the edits are stored in a digital format.

NONOBJECTIVE: Representing an object that is not seen or exist in the space shown.

OBSCENE: Depending on the location, obscene refers to material that is patently offensive to the public viewing the material. This decision has been defined by US court filings but is constantly under review and disagreement of the interpretation of the definition.

PACE: Is determined by the overall measurement of the perceived movement of the entire production.

PDA (Personal Digital Assistant): A small hand-held computer used to keep track of data and information during a shoot.

PERSISTENCE OF VISION: The physical effect of an image remaining on the retina of the eye for approximately 1/10 of a second.

PHENOMENA: An unusual occurrence or action, performance, or production, much beyond any expected normal standard.

PHONETICALLY: Analyzing the speech of a character in terms of the actual sound of the word, not how the word is spelled.

PHONETICS: The process of breaking down the actual sounds of a word regardless of the spelling to reach the basis for how that word is constructed for animation.

PHYSIOLOGY: The science of analyzing the basic of an item from a biological point of view.

PITCH SESSION: A meeting of an animator with a group of supporters, or funding sources to determine if the project is worthy for their support.

PORNOGRAPHIC: The legal judgment of medial that is not universally accepted on the basis of its depiction of sexual activities.

POTENTIAL: A possible action, but not necessarily an absolute confirmed action.

PRELIMINARY: The first or the very beginning of an action or movement.

PRE-VIZ: A preliminary tentative sample of a production to view for timing and accuracy in the animation and synchronization.

PROLIFIC: Producing an abundance of scenes, cells, frames, or files for a production, or a large number of copies for the same production.

PROPELS: To shoot or carry forward with force and direction.

PROTAGONIST: The main character in a story, usually the lead, hero or heroine, who sets the feel of the story. Usually in some type of conflict with the antagonist.

PULLDOWN: The method of converting a film signal to a digital file. Film frames are matched to digital by alternating between two film frames to either 2 or 3 digital fields per second. Film is exposed at 24 FPS (actually 23.976 FPS), and digital is 30 FPS (actually 29.97 FPS) or 60 FPS.

PUPPETS: Three-dimensional physical figures and objects designed with hinges, wires, and other supports allowing them to be moved as needed for stop-action animation.

RATE: It is the perceived movement of individual portions of any performance.

RENDERING: The final file consisting of a combination of all files to create a completed digital segment or production.

RETRIBUTION: Payment or back payment for as a punishment for a preceding event or action.

RFP (Request For Proposal): A statement that a production company asks for ideas and preliminary concepts in advance before signing a contract.

RHYTHM: The audience perceived the rhythm of a performance by variations in pace, tempo, and rate of individual portions of the performance.

ROTOSCOPE: The process of converting a live-action shot to animation drawings.

ROUGH PASS (also rough cut): Preliminary assembly set of key parts of a production.

SCI-FI (Science Fiction): The genre using preconceived notions of scientific aspects of life in the future as the basis for a production.

SEMANTIC: The study of the development and changes in words and the pronunciation of words.

SFX (Sound Effects, or Special Effects): The technic of creating sounds as needed for a production.

SILHOUETTE: A clear outline of a character or object showing the shape but not detail of either.

SLANG: Words and phrases that are arbitrarily peculiar to a single group.

SLICE: A method to determine if and where in a digital field there may be an error that may be avoided.

SOUND TRACK: The collection of all of the sounds used in a sequence, segment, or an entire production.

SOUND TREATMENT: A preliminary listing of all the sounds in a production, or an actual recording of all of the sounds planned for a production.

SPAM: Unwanted digital material, files, and websites.

STATIC: Unwanted sounds interfering with a sound track. Usually caused by adjacent high-level signals.

STEREOTYPE: Using the same information over and over without good reason. Also used to speak negatively of groups who are different from the speaker.

STOCK FOOTAGE: Files of digital sequences, film, or photos used to fill in gaps for a production.

STOP-ACTION: Producing an animation by shooting one frame at a time. Usually used for puppets, and hand-crafted items, or for removing certain frames from a live-action sequence.

STOP WATCH: A mechanism to mark accurate time sequences, frames, series of actions, or audio analysis of a sound track. May be either analog or digital or built into a digital app.

STORYLINE: A summary of the plot of a story, also sometimes labeled "The Premise".

SUBSERVIENT: A subordinate position of a crew member or cast.

SYNCHRONIZATION (Sync): The coordination of two production elements precisely matching the sound and the visual. Also may refer to a variety of actions that must be matched for the director's desired effect.

TEMPO: Use the perceived specific rate of movement of individual portions of a performance.

TEXTURE: The tactile surface of a wall, object, or costume.

THIRD PERSON: The third of the three pronouns, the first person is either I or We. The second person is you, and the third person is he, she, or they.

THUMBNAILS: Small drawings used as preliminary storyboards, flip books, or preliminary sketches of an aspect of a production.

VERTICAL: A line running from the top to the bottom of a chart or graph, also positing an object upright on its base or stand.

VIABLE: A proposal, concept, or sketch that offers the possibility to be acceptable or to be produced.

VISUALIZE: To be able to see in your own mind what you would like to create or so that others may also view the same object or animation.

VOICEOVER: The sound track made up of talent reading copy without being visible. Also, the process of adding copy after the visual has been completed.

VOWELS: The letters of the alphabet that are made with the mouth open: a, e, i, o, u.

XLR (Microsoft Excel): A writing app used for bookkeeping and other logging functions. Produced by Microsoft.

Animation Digital Sources

www.abc.com
www.aardman.com
www.adultswim.com
www.amazon.com
www.animationdirectory.ca
www.animationguild.org
www.animationnation.com
www.animationshow.com
www.animationsandtricks.com
www.animationusa.com
www.animationresources.org
www.asifa-hollywood.com
www.awn.com
www.awesomedudness.com
www.bitterfilms.com
www.blendfilms.com
www.cartoonnetwwork.com
www.channelfrederator.com
www.chuckjones.com
www.coldhardflash.com
www.comcentral.com
www.wbanimation.com
www.thedisneyblog.com

www.disneybooks.disney.go.com
www.dccomics.com
www.discovery.com
www.drawn.ca
www.fantagraphics.com
www.gabocorp.com
www.jimhillmedia.com
www.michaelspornanimation.com
www.mtv.com
www.newsfromme.com
www.nick.com
www.nonstick.com
www.pbs.org
www.robedwards.net/
www.spikeandmike.com
www.texavery.com
www.tnt-tv.com
www.tv.warnerbros.com
www.wordomatic.blogspot.com
www.vintageip.com
www.weblogs.variety.com/
  bags_and_boards

Bibliography

Anderson, John and Barbara Anderson. The myth of persistence of vision revisited. *Journal of Film and Video* 1993; 45(1), 2–12.

Arnheim, Rudolph. *Film as Art*. Berkeley, CA: University of California Press, 1971.

Bancroft, Tony. *Directing for Animation: Everything You Did Not Learn in Art School*. Boston, MA: Focal Press, 2014.

Barrier, Michael. *Hollywood Cartoons: American Animation in Its Golden Age*. Oxford : Oxford University Press, 1999.

Bauder, Irv. *Screenwriting Fundamentals: The Art and Craft of Visual Writing*. London, UK: Routledge, 2017.

Bazin, Andre. *What is Cinema?* Vol. I (Trans. Hugh Gray). Berkeley, CA: University of California Press, 1971.

Beck, Jerry, ed. *Animation from Pencil to Pixel: The History of Cartoons, Anime, and CGI*. New York: Harper Collins, 2004.

Beckerman, Howard. *Animation: The Whole Story*, revised edn. New York: Allworth Press, 2003.

Beiman, Nancy. *Prepare to Board! Creating Story and Characters for Animated Features and Shorts*, 3rd edn. Boca Raton, FL: Taylor & Francis, 2017.

Bendazzi, Giannalberto. *Cartoons: One Hundred Years of Cinema Animation*. Bloomington, IN: University of Indiana Press, 1995.

Bird, Brad. DVD Commentary on the Animation feature: *The Incredibles*, 2004.

Bousquet, Michele. *Physics for Animators*. Boston, MA: Focal Press, 2016.

Cavalier, Stephen. *The World History of Animation*. Berkeley, CA: University of California Press, 2011.

Ceram, C. W. *Archaeology of the Cinema*. (Trans. Richard Winston). New York: Harcourt, Brace & World, Inc., 1965.

Cholodenko, Alan, ed. *The Illusion of Life: Essays on Animation*. Sydney, Australia: Power Publications, 1991.

Cholodenko, Alan. The animator is artist, the artist as animator. *Animation Studies Online Journal*, 2015.

Crafton, Donald. *Before Mickey: The Animated Film 1898–1928*. Chicago, IL: The University of Chicago Press, 1993.

Dickson, William K. and Antonia Dickson. *History of the Kinetograph, Kinetoscope and Kineto-Phonograph*. New York: Albert Bunm, Imprimatur, 1895. Facsimile Reprint, New York: Museum of Modern Art, 2001.

Eisenstein, Sergei. *Film Form Film Sense*. (Trans. Jay Leyda). New York: Meridian Books, 1957.

Engler, Robi. *Animation Cinema Workshop: From Motion to Emotion*. Indianapolis, IN: John Libbey Publishing, 2016.

Enticknap, Leo. *Moving Image Technology: From Zoetrope to Digital*. London: Wallflower Press, 2005.

Furniss, Maureen. *Art in Motion: Animation Aesthetics*. Sydney, Australia: John Libbey & Co., 1998.

Furniss, Maureen. *A New History of Animation*. New York: Thames & Hudson, 2016.

Ghertne, ed. *Layout and Composition for Animation*. Boston, MA: Focal Press, 2011.

Giannakopoulas Theodoros and Aggelos Pikrakis. *Introduction to Audio Analysis*. Atlanta, GA: Academic Press, 2014.

Goldberg, Eric. *Character Animation Crash Course!*. Los Angeles, CA: Simon-James Press, 2008.

Goulekas, Karen E. *Visual Effects in a Digital World: A Glossary of Visual Effects Terms*. San Francisco, CA: Harcourt, 2001.

Green, Garo and James C., Kaufman. *Video Games and Creativity*. Atlanta, GA: Academic Press, 2015.

Halas, John. *Timing for Animation*. Boston, MA: Focal Press, 2009.

Halas, John and Roger Manvell. *The Technique of Film Animation*, 7th edn. New York: Hasting House, 1973.

Hart, John. *The Art of the Storyboard: Storyboarding for Film, TV, and Animation*. Boston, MA: Focal Press, 1999.

Henderson, Donald. *Creators of Life: A History of Animation*. New York: Drake Publishers, 1975.

Hoffer, Thomas W. *Animation: A Reference Guide*. Westport, CN: Greenwood Press, 1981.

Holman, L. Bruce. *Puppet Animation in the Cinema: History and Technique*. New York: A. S. Barnes and Company, 1975.

Holman, Tomlinson. *Sound for Digital Video*. Boston, MA: Focal Press, 2005.

Iwerks, Leslie and John Kenworthy. *The Hand Behind the Mouse: An Intimate Biography of Ub Iwerks, the Man Walt Disney Called "The Greatest Animator in the World."* New York: Disney Editions, 2001.

Janson, H. W. *History of Art: A Survey of the Major Visual Arts from the Dawn of History to the Present Day*, 2nd edn. New York: Harry N Abrams, 1978.

Jones, Angie and Jamie Oliff. *Thinking Animation: Bridging the Gap Between 2D and CG*. Independence, KY: Thomson, 2007.

Jones, Chuck. *Chuck Amuck: The Life and Times of an Animated Cartoonist*. New York: Farrar Straus Giroux, 1989.

Jones, Chuck. *Chuck Jones' Chuck Reducks: Drawing from the Fun Side of Life*. New York: Warner Books, 1996.

Jones, Chuck. *The Paradoxes of Art: A Phenomenological Investigation*, by Alan Paskow, Cambridge: Cambridge University Press, 2002, 260 pp.

Kerlow, Isaac Victor. *The Art of 3D Computer Animation and Effects*, 4th edn. Hoboken, NJ: John Wiley & Sons, 2004.

Kohlers, Paul A. The illusion of movement. *Scientific American* 1964; 211, 12.

Krasner, Jon. *Motion Graphic Design Fine Art Animation.* Boston, MA: Focal Press, 2004.

Kuperberg, Marcia. *A Guide to Computer Animation: For TV, Games, Multimedia, and Web.* Woburn, MA: Focal Press, 2002.

Lasseter, John. A minute with Disney's John Lasseter on creating Oscar magic. UK Edition off Reuters. *Entertainment News,* February 25, 2010.

Laybourne, Kit. *The Animation Book: New Digital Edition.* New York: Three Rivers Press, 1998.

Lenburg, Jeff. *The Great Cartoon Directors.* New York: Da Capo Press, 1993.

Lumiere, Louis. The Lumiere cinematograph. *SMPTE Journal* 1996; 105, 608–611.

Lutz, E. G. *Animated Cartoons: How They Are Made, Their Origin and Development,* Originally published, New York: Charles Scribner's Sons, 1920. Reprinted, Bedford, MA: Applewood Books, 1998. (Note: The original of this book, published in 1925, was the book Disney used to learn how to animate his first shorts.)

Lye, Len. "The Art that Moves", in *Figures of Motion: Len Lye/Selected Writings.* Auckland: Auckland University Press, 1964, p. 82.

Maltin, Leonard. *Of Mice and Magic: A History of American Animated Cartoons,* revised edn. New York, Plume Books, 1987.

Manovich, Lev. *Post-Cinema Theorizing 21st-Century Film.* Falmer: REFRAME Books, 2016.

Mattesi, Mike, *Force: Dynamic Life Drawing,* 10th edn. Boca Raton, FL: CRC Press, 2017.

McKim, Robert H. *Experiences in Visual Thinking.* Monterey, CA: Brooks/Cole, 1972.

Menache, Alberto. *Understanding Motion Capture for Computer Animation,* 2nd edn. Atlanta, GA: Elsevier, 2010.

Mitchell, Ben. *Independent Animation: Developing, Producing and Distributing Your Animated Films.* Boca Raton, FL: CRC Press, 2016.

Movshovitz, Dean. *Pixar Storytelling: Rules for Effective Storytelling Based on Pixar's Greatest Films.* North Charlette, SC: CreateSpace Independent Publishing, 2015.

Noake, Roger. *Animation Techniques: Planning and Producing Animation with Today's Technologies.* Secausun, NJ: Chartwell Books, Inc., 1988.

O'Hailey, Tina. *Hybrid Animation: Integrating 2D and 3D Assets.* Boston, MA: Focal Press, 2015.

Patmore, Chris. *The Complete Animation: The Principles, Practices, Techniques of Successful Animation.* Haupauge, NY: Barrons, 2003.

Plympton, Bill. *Hair High (A graphic novel of the motion picture of the same name).* New York: NBM Publishing, 2003.

Rabiger, Michael. *Developing Story Ideas,* 3rd edn. Boston, MA: Focal Press, 2017.

Roberts, Steve. *Character Animation Fundamentals. Developing Skills for 2D and 3D Character Animation.* Boston, MA: Focal Press, 2012.

Russett, Robert and Cecile Starr. *Experimental Animation: An Illustrated Anthology.* New York: Van Nostrand Reinhold, 1976.

Russett, Robert and Cecile Starr. *Experimental Animation: Origins of a New Art.* New York: Da Capo Press, (Reprint) 1976.

Shaw, Susannah. *Stop Motion: Craft Skills for Model Animation,* 3rd edn. Boston, MA: Focal Press, 2017.

Sito, Tom. *Drawing the Line: The Untold Story of the Animation Unions from Bosko to Bart Simpson*, Lexington, KY: Kentucky University Press, 2006.

Solomon, Charles. *The History of Animation: Enchanted Drawings*. San Antonio, TX: Wings Books, 1994.

Stanchfield, Walt. *Drawn to Life: 20 Golden Years of Disney Master Classes, Vol. 1 & Vol. 2*. (Don Hahn, ed.) Boston, MA: Focal Press, 2009.

Stephenson, Ralph. *The Animated Film,* New York: A.S. Barnes, 1973.

Subotnick, Steve. *Animation in the Home Digital Studio: Creation to Distribution*. Boston, MA: Focal Press, 2003.

Taylor, Richard. *Encyclopedia of Animation Techniques*. Philadelphia, PA: Running Press Book Publishers, 1996.

Webster, Chris. *The Mechanics of Motion*. Boston, MA: Focal Press, 2005.

Webster, Chris. *Action Analysis for Animators*. Boston, MA: Focal Press, 2012.

Wells, Paul. *Understanding Animation*. London: Routledge, 1998.

Wells, Paul. *Animation and America*. New Brunswick, NJ: Rutgers University Press, 2002.

White, Tony. *Animation from Pencil top Pixels*. Woburn, MA: Focal Press, 2006.

White, Tony. *The Animator's Sketchbook: How to See, Interpret & Draw Like a Master Animator*. Boca Raton, FL: CRC Press. 2016.

Williams, Richard. *The Animator's Survival Kit*, 4th edn. New York: Farrar, Straus, and Giroux, 2012.

Winder, Catherine and Zahra Dowlatabadi. *Producing Animation*. Boston, MA: Focal Press, 2001.

Winters, Patrick. *Sound Design for Low and NO Budget Films*. London, UK: Routledge, 2017.

Woolery, George W. *Children's Television: The First Thirty-Five Years, 1946–1981*. Metuchen, NJ: The Scarecrow Press, 1983.

Wright, Jean A. *Animation Writing and Development: From Script Development to Pitch*. Boston, MA: Focal Press, 2005.

Zettl, Herbert. *Sight Sound Motion*, 4th edn. Belmont, CA: Wadsworth Publishing, 2005.

Index